Also by Adrien Fontanellaz: *A@W* Volumes 23 & 24

Also by Tom Cooper: *A@W* Volumes 13, 14, 18, 19, 21, 23 & 24

Published in 2018 by:
Helion & Company Limited
26 Willow Road
Solihull
West Midlands
B91 1UE
England
Tel. 0121 705 3393
Fax 0121 711 4075
email: info@helion.co.uk
website: www.helion.co.uk
Twitter: @helionbooks
Visit our blog http://blog.helion.co.uk/

Text © Adrien Fontanellaz and Tom Cooper
    2018
Maps drawn by George Anderson © Helion
& Company 2018
Photographs © as individually credited
Colour profiles © Tom Cooper / David
Bocquelet 2017, as indicated

Designed & typeset by Farr out Publications,
    Wokingham, Berkshire
Cover design by Paul Hewitt, Battlefield
    Design (www.battlefield-design.co.uk)
Printed by Henry Ling Ltd, Dorchester,
    Dorset

ISBN 978-1-912390-29-8

British Library Cataloguing-in-Publication
    Data
A catalogue record for this book is available
    from the British Library

CONTENTS

Note: In order to simplify the use of this book, all names, locations and geographic designations are as provided in *The Times World Atlas*, or other traditionally accepted major sources of reference, as of the time of described events.

ACKNOWLEDGMENTS

This book is a result of cooperation with a number of individuals from the Horn of Africa, who generously helped with background and insider knowledge, relevant information, and expertise; foremost Maj Gen Ashenafi Gebre Tsadik (EtAF ret.) and Col Berhanu Wubneh (EtAF ret.). While establishing contact with them and prompting them to share their recollections proved a very complex and problematic task, there is little doubt that it would have been impossible to realize this project without their kind help and patience. Not a few others have initially refused any kind of contact, but eventually agreed to grant verbal or written narratives solely on condition of absolute anonymity – for reasons of concerns for their own, and the safety of their families. We would like to express our special gratitude to everybody involved, but also to promise to keep the memory of a number of persons that have passed away in the meantime, or those that are in poor health now.

Fortunately, the Ethiopian military history was meanwhile extensively studied by native academic researchers who produced several seminal works based on documentation from official archives. In particular, works by Fantahun Ayele and Gebru Tareke made the coming-into-being of our research possible.

We would also like to thank to Dan Connell, who has made numerous journeys to Eritrea since the 1970s and published several books about his experiences, and kindly allowed us to use his pictures; Albert Grandolini and Jacques Guillem from France; Pit Weinert from Germany; Jeroen Nijmeijer from The Netherlands; Mark Lepko and Tom Long from the USA for providing extensive aid in photographic, and other forms of research, that eventually made this book possible.

ABBREVIATIONS

AAA	Anti-Aircraft Artillery
AA-2 Atoll	ASCC code for R-3S or R-13, Soviet air-to-air missile
AB	Air Base
AdA	Armée de l'Air (French Air Force)
AK	Russian for Automat Kalashnikova; general designation for a class of Soviet – or former East Block-manufactured class of 7.^{62}mm assault rifles
An	Antonov (the design bureau led by Oleg Antonov)
APC	Armoured Personnel Carrier
ASCC	Air Standardisation Co-ordinating Committee (US, British, Australian and New Zealand committee for standardisation of designations of foreign aircraft)
CAP	combat air patrol
Capt	Captain (military commissioned officer rank)
CAS	close air support
CAdS	Corpo Aeronautico della Somalia (Somali Aeronautical Corps)
CBU	cluster bomb unit
CCS	Ciidanka Cirka Soomaliaayed (Somali Air Force)
C-in-C	Commander-in-Chief
CO	Commanding Officer
COIN	counterinsurgency
CPSU	Communist Party of the Soviet Union
DAAFAR	Defesa Anti-Aérea y Fuerza Aérea Revolucionaria (Cuban Air Defence Force & Air Force; often shortened to 'FAR' in every-day conversation)
DoD	Department of Defence (USA)
EAL	Ethiopian Airlines
EDU	Ethiopian Democratic Union
EE	English Electric
ELA	Eritrean Liberation Army
ELF	Eritrean Liberation Front
ELINT	Electronic intelligence
EPLA	Eritrean People's Liberation Army
EPLF	Eritrean People's Liberation Front
EPRDF	Ethiopian People's Revolutionary Democratic Front
EtAF	Ethiopian Air Force
Flg Off	Flight Officer (military commissioned officer rank, equal to Lieutenant or 1st Lieutenant)
Flt Lt	Flight Lieutenant (military commissioned officer rank, equal to Captain)
FS	Fighter Squadron
GCI	ground control/ed interception
Gen	General (military commissioned officer rank)
GP	General-purpose (bomb)
HE	high explosive
HQ	headquarters
IAI	Israeli Aircraft Industries (since 2006 Israeli Aerospace Industries)
IAP	International Airport
IDF	Israeli Defence Force
IEA	Imperial Ethiopian Aviation
IEAF	Imperial Ethiopian Air Force
IEAA	Imperial Ethiopian Army Aviation
IFF	Identification Friend or Foe
IFV	Infantry fighting vehicle
IR	Infra-red, electromagnetic radiation longer than deepest red light sensed as heat
Il	Ilyushin (the design bureau led by Sergey Vladimirovich Ilyushin, also known as OKB-39)
IIAF	Imperial Iranian Air Force
IRIAF	Islamic Republic of Iran Air Force
KGB	Komitet Gosudarstvennoy Bezopasnosti (Committee for State Security – Soviet National Security Agency, 1954-1991)
KIA	killed in action

Km	kilometre
MAAG	Military Aid and Assistance Group
MANPAD(S)	man-portable air defence system(s) – light surface-to-air missile system that can be carried and deployed in combat by a single soldier
MBT	Main Battle Tank
Mi	Mil (Soviet/Russian helicopter designer and manufacturer)
MIA	missing in action
MiG	Mikoyan i Gurevich (the design bureau led by Artyom Ivanovich Mikoyan and Mikhail Iosifovich Gurevich, also known as OKB-155 or MMZ' "Zenit")
MoD	Ministry of Defence
MONPC	Military Operations and National Planning Command
MRL	multiple rocket launcher
NCO	Non-commissioned officer
OAU	Organisation of African Unity
OLF	Oromo Liberation Front
PDRYAF	People's Democratic Republic of Yemen Air Force (air force of former South Yemen)
PLO	Palestinian Liberation Organization
PMAC	Provisional Military Administrative Committee (120-member committee of Ethiopian officers, better known as the 'Derg' or 'Dergue')
PoW	Prisoner of War
R-3S	Soviet-made air-to-air missile (see AA-2)
RA	Regia Aeronautica (Royal Italian Air Force)
RAF	Royal Air Force
RHAW	Radar homing and warning system
RWR	Radar Warning Receiver
SA-2 Guideline	ASCC code for S-75 Dvina, Soviet SAM system

SA-3 Goa	ASCC code for S-125 Neva, Soviet SAM system
SA-7 Grail	ASCC code for 9K32 Strela-2, Soviet MANPAD
SA-13	ASCC code for Strela-10, Soviet SAM system
SAAB	Svenska Aeroplan Aktiebolaget (Swedish aircraft manufacturer)
SAC	Somali Aeronautical Corps
SALF	Somali-Abo Liberation Front
SAM	surface-to-air missile
SMSC	Supreme Military Strategic Committee
SNA	Somali National Army
SNDF	Somali National Defence Force
Sqn	Squadron
Sqn Ldr	Squadron Leader (military commissioned officer rank, equal to Major)
TPLA	Tigrayan People's Liberation Army
TPLF	Tigrayan People's Liberation Front
UN	United Nations
UNHCR	UN High Commissioner for Refugees
UNRWA	United Nations Relief and Works Agency
USAAF	United States Army Air Force (until 1947)
USAF	United States Air Force (since 1947)
US$	United States Dollar
USSR	Union of Soviet Socialist Republics
V-TA	Komandovaniye voyenno-transportnoy aviatsii (Soviet Military Transport Aviation)
V-VS	Voyenno-Vozdushnye Sily (Soviet Air Force)
WIA	Wounded in Action
WSLF	Western Somali Liberation Front
WWI	World War I
WWII	World War II

ADDENDA TO AFRICA@WAR 18: WINGS OVER OGADEN, THE ETHIOPIAN-SOMALI WAR 1978-79

While no new information surfaced in reaction to volume 18 of this series, sources in Ethiopia went to great extents to obtain and provide better scans of several highly valuable photographs. These are enclosed for readers' interest.

This is one of only two Northrop F-5B two-seat conversion trainers delivered to Ethiopia in the late 1960s. Like the rest of the fleet, they were painted in silver grey on delivery. Notable is that this aircraft remained in service long enough to receive national markings introduced in 1978 – including a five-pointed yellow star. (EtAF via S.N.)

This is, so far, the best photograph available showing the F-5E with serial number 430. It is showing six 'kill markings', in form of blue stars applied on the side of the fuselage, below the cockpit. Contrary to usual practice in other air forces, these were attached in form of metal stars bolted on the aircraft's skin. Notable is that by the time it received kill markings, 430 has also got the national insignia in form of a five-pointed star, applied in 1978. (EtAF via S. N.)

Apparently taken shortly after arrival of F-5Es in Ethiopia in 1976. This photograph shows the Tiger II with serial number 431. Except for this aircraft, and above-mentioned 430, other F-5Es known to have been in service during the Ogaden War wore serials 418, 419, and 429. (Pit Weinert Collection)

Following one operational loss and one defection during the Ogaden War, 44th Squadron EtAF was down to only two Canberras. Their serial numbers were 351 and 353. This undated photograph shows 351 to advantage. (EtAF via S. N.)

CHAPTER 1
SUNSET OF THE TRADITIONAL ETHIOPIAN MILITARY

For much of the 1980s, reports surfaced in the Western media time and again about a little known, yet particularly bitter, war on the African Horn. Apparently, there was an uprising in north-eastern Ethiopia, where locals launched a major insurgency against the military of what, at that time, was perceived as a 'Soviet-supported regime' in Addis Ababa. On its own, this was nothing new, because reports about local uprisings, military coups and other kind of political unrest in Ethiopia were quite frequent since earlier times. However, the war of the 1980s did appear different because some of the reports indicated a massive deployment of air power and mechanized military formations.

Related reporting nearly stopped in 1989 when the government of the Union of the Soviet Socialist Republics (USSR or Soviet Union) announced it would cease supporting the Ethiopian government. Less than two years later, dramatic photographs and news surfaced about insurgents entering the Ethiopian capital and toppling the government.

A few years later, several larger publications appeared describing dramatic, large-scale battles fought between Eritreans and Ethiopians, and even citing some 'thrilling' code-names for specific operations, such as 'Red Star' for example. With the advent of the internet, photographs began surfacing showing seemingly endless 'killing fields': entire columns of Soviet-made tanks and other equipment destroyed, twisted, burned and now forlorn on former battlefields of what were obviously pitched battles.

In 1998 a new war erupted, this time pitting the large armies of Eritrea and Ethiopia against one another, in what was the last conventional conflict of the 20th – but also the first of the 21st – Century. This time, rumours began spreading about even bigger battles, deployment of some of most modern military technology of Russian origin, and air battles between such advanced fighter-bomber types as Mikoyan i Gurevich MiG-29 and Sukhoi Su-27.

Nevertheless, through all of this time very few hard facts became known about what exactly happened before, and during, two obviously massive conflicts between Ethiopia and Eritrea.

ndeed, for many interested foreign observers, it appeared de-facto impossible that two nations, widely considered as some of the poorest on the African continent, could have run military conflicts of the reported size and scope.

This view began to change only over the last decade, when the first authoritative accounts were published – foremost by Ethiopian researchers like Fantahun Ayele and Gebru Tareke. Rather suddenly they provided an image of the constantly growing Ethiopian military of the 1980s and its involvement in a massive, decades-long, war against an uprising in Eritrea. This was far from all: through such publications it became obvious that the conflict fought between 1961-1991, nowadays colloquially known as the Eritrean Liberation War, included a full spectrum of warfare: from almost classic, so-called counter-insurgency (COIN) operations, via mechanized warfare in the desert, to conventional mountain warfare. Furthermore, it became known that the campaigns of this war were often conducted by powerful, comparatively well-equipped forces, led by well-educated commanders that followed carefully designed military plans – even if operating on the basis of what was largely a home-grown doctrine.

As Ethiopia gradually re-built its military – especially during the so-called Badme War with Eritrea, fought in 1998-2001 – and then became involved in fighting in ruined Somalia too, it became obvious that this country is a military powerhouse of the African continent. This made it even more important to study not only the performance of its military in the course of earlier wars, but the influence of earlier military traditions and military history in general upon modern-day military thinking in the country too. It was for this reason that we have decided to include a chapter dedicated to the Italian invasion of Ethiopia in 1935 and its aftermath – to show how the Ethiopian feudal armies fought, and how at least similar tactics remained influential until recent times. Namely, that tactics were the core reason why such insurgent movements, like those in Eritrea and Tigray of the 1980s, virtually devoid of external support, not only developed in imposing fashion but also developed astonishing skills in the conduct of manoeuvring warfare in mountainous terrain.

The following volume is the result of all these years of – often troublesome – research about related issues. The narrative it offers is based on information from very different sources. Works by Ethiopian scholars like Ayele and Tareke were crucial, perhaps to the degree of actually making it possible. However, other sources – including some of Ethiopian participants in these wars – became available over time too. Even with all of their help, some details – especially those related to the Badme War – remain unknown. Due to multiple ongoing tensions on the internal and international plan alike, this is unlikely to change in the foreseeable future.

Geography

Situated at the north-eastern corner of Africa close to the Arabian Peninsula, and on the coast of the Indian Ocean, the Gulf of Aden, and the Red Sea, and containing ports and airfields that connect routes of intercontinental significance, the Horn of Africa is of significant strategic importance.

Stretching from Sudan in the north and west, southwards to Kenya, and to Djibouti in the east, Ethiopia is the biggest country in this area. More than half of Ethiopian territory is covered by the Ethiopian Plateau, diagonally split in a north-eastern to south-eastern direction by the Great Rift Valley, and with an average elevation of about 1,680m above the sea level. The plateau is cut by many rivers and deep valleys, ranging from the Dallow Depression, 100m below

the sea level, to the South Mountains of the central highlands that raise 4,000m high. The south of Ethiopia is bisected by the 40-60km wide Rift Valley. The road network remains underdeveloped, and in many areas is actually non-existent, significantly impeding vehicular movement during rainy seasons – the principal of which occurs between mid-June and September, followed by a dry season that may be interrupted by a short rainy season in February or March.

Although largely homogenous in regards of religion, the population of Ethiopia is deeply divided along ethnic, regional, and political lines, and the country faced an uphill struggle in keeping all of these united for centuries. The Amhara, who founded the original nation, and the related Tigreans, both of whom are highland peoples of partly Semitic origin, constitute around 30% of the total population. They primarily occupy the north-western Ethiopian highlands and the area north of Addis Ababa. Central and south-western Ethiopia is largely populated by the Oromo, a pastoral and agricultural people that constitute up to 40% of the nation's population. Western Ethiopia is predominantly populated by the Shankella, who constitute about 6% of the population, while the east and southeast is predominantly populated by the Somali. Out of around 70 languages spoken in Ethiopia, most belong to the Semitic and Cushitic branches of Afro-Asiatic family. Amharic, the official language, is spoken by more than half of the population, but English and Arabic are spoken by many too.

Nowadays, Ethiopia is divided into nine regions that have a significant degree of autonomy and are composed around specific ethnic groups: Tigray, Afar, Oromia, Somalia, Benshangul-Gumaz, Gamela, Harar, and the Southern Nations, Nationalities and Peoples, which comprises about 41 different ethnic groups. Addis Ababa is the largest city, but only about 15-20% of the population can be classified as 'urban'.

About 40% of Ethiopians are Christians, primarily followers of the Ethiopian Orthodox Union church, an autonomous Christian sect headed by a patriarch and closely related to the Coptic church of Egypt (which was the state church of Ethiopia until 1974). All the southern and eastern regions have Muslim majorities, who represent about 45% of the country's population. The south also contains considerable numbers of animists, while the majority of members of the sect known as Beta Israel, or Falashas, who practiced a type of Judaism - that probably dates back to contact with early Arabian Jews - were airlifted to Israel in 1991.

The economy is heavily dependent on the earnings of the agricultural sector, with raising of livestock being the most characteristic form of economic activity, followed by farming of coffee, cotton, sugar, fruit and vegetables, but much trading is conducted by barter in local markets, especially because periodic droughts have greatly reduced agricultural output and repeatedly forced the country to import basic foodstuffs.

Ethiopian Origins

Ethiopia is a country situated in one of the oldest – if not the oldest – area of human habitation. Archaeological research has proved that the modern homo sapiens probably evolved there. The original form of the modern-day name of this country was first used by ancient Greeks to refer to the peoples living south of ancient Egypt; modern usage has transferred this name further south, to the land of people known until the early 20th Century as Abyssinia.

In the 1st Century AD, the Axumite Empire developed in the area. Relatively isolated due to inaccessibility of the high central plateau, rich with gold, iron and salt deposits, it eventually became one of the five largest empires of the world in its time. It was in

British troops during the 'Abbisinian Expedition' in 1868. (National Museum of Ethiopia)

the year 330 that it experienced the introduction of Christianity through the Greek clergy. Through the following two centuries, the Axumite Empire benefited from a major transformation of the maritime trading system that linked the Roman Empire and India. This increased the significance of the Red Sea as a trading route that made Axum's main port, Adulis, a major trading centre. At its height, the Axumite Empire controlled the area covering the entire modern-day Ethiopia, Eritrea, northern Sudan, southern Egypt, Djibouti, Yemen and southern Arabia.

Axum remained strong until the rise of Islam in the 7th Century. Because the Axumites had sheltered Muhammad's first followers, the Muslims never attempted to conquer the country as they spread across Africa. While the Axumite naval power gradually declined through that period, in 702 its pirates were able to invade the Hejaz and occupy Jeddah. In retaliation, Muslims took the Dahlak Archipelago from Axum and began spreading along the coast of the Red Sea, forcing Axum into isolation from the rest of the world.

In the medieval ages, three chief provinces came into being: Tigray in the north, Amhara in the centre, and Shewa in the south. The seat of the government was usually in Amhara, but at times there were two, or even three, kings reigning at the same time. It was only in 1528 that Ethiopia again made contact with the outside world. Invaded by a Muslim army from the nearby Sultanate of Adal, the Negus ('King') Lebna Dengle Dawit II requested help from Portugal. As the Muslim force came close to extinguishing the ancient realm of Ethiopia and converting all of its subjects to Islam, the Portuguese expedition led by Cristóvão da Gama arrived in 1541, and saved the nation, but was subsequently obliged to make their way out of Ethiopia and the areas that are nowadays part of Somalia.

Many historians trace the origins of hostility between Ethiopia and Somalia to this war, but the conflict of 1528-1541 also resulted in bitter religious conflicts with the Jesuits and inner struggles between different Ethiopian rulers, and the country remained relatively isolated for the following 300 years. It was not before 1855, when Lij Kassa proclaimed himself 'Negus Negusti' ('King of Kings') under the name of Tewodros II and launched a campaign to unite the nation under his rule, that the modernisation and opening of Ethiopia began. Although a ruthless ruler, Tewodros was determined to protect the country from the Europeans who were scrambling to get colonies in Africa at that time. When Queen Victoria failed to answer his letter, in 1867, he took it an insult and

imprisoned several British residents, including the consul. The British deployed an army of 12,000 from Mumbai to Ethiopia and defeated Tewodros during the battle at Magdala (better known as Amba Mariam), prompting him into a suicide.

Emergence of Eritrea

The end of Tewodros' rule resulted in an internal power struggle won by Kassa, who was crowned as the Emperor Yohannes IV, and rose to power at the time that the area of the Red Sea became strategically important due to the opening of the Suez Canal. As Western colonial nations opened political battles for the control over the shores, the British occupied Yemen, the French took Obock Asars and Issa, while Ethiopians had the ambition to conquer the source of the Nile and invaded Sudan. In 1870, the Italians appeared on the scene, buying the port of Asseb from the local sultan. In 1888, the Italians exploited Yohannes IV's preoccupation with defending Ethiopia from an invasion of dervishes from Sudan, and deployed 20,000 troops in the country. Not interested in fighting the newcomers, the emperor solved all the disputes – more or less – through negotiations, and granted permission for some 5,000 troops to remain stationed in a part of the Ethiopian Tigray Province, which over the time became known as 'Eritrea'.

Meanwhile, on 9 March 1889, Yohannes IV defeated the Dervish invasion, but a stray bullet hit him and his army withdrew. The Emperor died during the night and his body fell into the hands of the enemy. As soon as this news reached Sahle Maryam of Shewa, he proclaimed himself Emperor Menelik II of Ethiopia. Only two months later, Menelik II signed a treaty with Rome, granting Eritrea to Italy in exchange for supply of 30,000 rifles, ammunition and several cannons. The Italians scrambled to declare this treaty as granting them a protectorate over all of Ethiopia, causing Menelik's protests that were completely ignored, and leading to another war. The following conflict between Ethiopia and Italy culminated in a humiliating Italian defeat during the battle of Adwa, on 1 March 1896, and a provisional treaty of peace concluded at Addis Ababa, with which Rome recognized the absolute independence of Ethiopia, and thus became the first internationally recognized independent African state.[1]

Following this success, the Ethiopians invested heavily in development of modern infrastructure, including the construction of the Addis Ababa-Djibouti railroad, and post and telephone services.[2] The emperor began appointing ministers, a bank was founded, and the first hotel, hospitals, and schools opened in the capital.

Menelik died in December 1913 and was succeeded by his grandson, who proved unpopular due to ties to Muslims, and ruled only for three years. In 1916 he was deposed by the Christian nobility that made Menelik's daughter, Zauditu, empress, with her cousin Ras Tafari Mekonnen (son of a hero for the Battle of Adwa) regent and successor to the throne. After the death of Empress Zauditu in 1930, Mekonnen founded his own army and established himself in power, after a civil war, resulting in his crowning as Emperor Haile Selassie I of Ethiopia.

Modernisation of the Ethiopian Military

The primary reason for the Ethiopian success against the Italians during the battle of Adwa were the efforts of Emperors like Tewodros II, Yohannes IV, and Menelik II to modernize the Ethiopian military. Tewodros II in particular hired several Europeans to establish a foundry and produce mortars. Generally the results of such attempts were disappointing, and all experiments of that kind were short

An Ethiopian painting depicting the Battle of Adwa, in 1896. (National Museum of Ethiopia)

lived. Menelik II re-launched corresponding efforts and managed to obtain modern mountain guns. Correspondingly, he established a regular corps of uniformed gunners and then recruited at least one European to create workshops in Addis Ababa, where small arms ammunition was produced, and most rifles and guns could be overhauled. Finally, he inaugurated the War Ministry in 1907.[3]

Nevertheless, it was only under the future emperor Haile Selassie that a permanent body of soldiers, wearing uniforms and equipped with modern firearms, appeared in 1917. Selassie also took care to have a group of young men sent to France for education at the Military Academy of Saint Cyr. On their return, in 1928, they were organized into the Imperial Bodyguard. A year later, a Belgian military mission was established that remained in the country until 1935. Meanwhile, eager to obtain support from foreign powers that had no stake in Ethiopia, Selassie sent further cadets for training in France, and requested help from Sweden in 1934. A small team of Swedish instructors arrived in 1934 and helped establish the Holeta Military Training School. Together with other efforts, this enabled an expansion of the Imperial Bodyguard from 2,250 officers and other ranks in 1933, to 5,000 - organized into four battalions, a machine-gun company, and a cavalry squadron - in 1935.[4]

Furthermore, Selassie took steps to establish a small flying arm, equipped with aircraft that could be used for reconnaissance and liaison duties.[5]

The Ethiopian Military of the 1930s

Regardless of their significance, efforts to reform and modernize their state by various Ethiopian emperors were only partially successful, and this was nowhere as obvious as in regards of the Ethiopian military of the 1930s. Organized along traditional patterns, this consisted of the Emperor's own force – the Mahal Safari (which was also the only one to benefit from at least partial equipment with modern arms) – and a number of units maintained on permanent basis by various nobles (among which the Ras were the most powerful). Most of this army was composed of infantry, but it did include a light cavalry element, primarily drawn from

Troops of the Ethiopian Imperial Guard with a machine gun. As of the mid-1930s, they were the only uniformed soldiers in Ethiopia. (National Museum of Ethiopia)

Oromo.

Roughly comparable to the mobilisation systems from feudal Europe of earlier centuries, such an organisation offered the advantage of the ability to raise hundreds of thousands of fighters on relatively short notice.

Once deployed in field, the traditional Ethiopian army was always divided into a vanguard, two wings, and the main body. On advancing, each of its columns was further broken down into a vanguard, the main body divided into two wings, support units and the rear guard. Over time, indigenous military ranks developed accordingly. These included Fitaurari ('commander of the advance guard'), Cagnasmacc ('commander of the right wing'), Grassmacc ('commander of the left wing') and Asmacc ('commander of the rearguard').[6]

The strategy of the Ethiopian military was to seek decisive battles and to destroy the enemy with one blow with its own, highly effective tactics. Correspondingly, the Ethiopians sought to quickly engage the enemy force with the vanguard, while outflanking it before launching mass attacks against its weakest point. In the course of their mass charges, the Ethiopian warriors sought to close

Typical Oromo warrior of the 1930s. (NME)

the range and engage the enemy in hand-to-hand combat. Because of this, even fighters armed with rifles carried their shields and short swords.[8]

With Ethiopian military traditions being some of the oldest on this planet (they can be traced directly back to the Kingdom of Aksum's rise, in 1st Century BC), and due to constant warfare ever since, Ethiopian soldiers were highly motivated and willing to fight.[9]

Several of the foreign observers that witnessed the operations of the Ethiopian military during the late 19th and early 20th Century, tended to compare its discipline, organization and tactics with those of various European militaries. For example, Gerhard Kholfs, a German traveller who passed Ethiopia during the 19th Century, wrote:

> One must admit that the discipline in this primitive army is excellent.[10]

Similarly, General Ellna, one of Italian officers present in Adwa 1896, recalled:

> The Abyssinian tactics are admirable. The soldiers are well disciplined and always attack when they are certain to meet success. Their outflanking moves are unstoppable because of their speed.

However, the 'feudal' organization, strategy and tactics of the Ethiopian military had a number of drawbacks. They were heavily dependent on the loyalty of regional leaders, and produced a military that was not particularly homogenous because some formations were better armed than others. Foremost, its logistics system was most rudimentary and the field organization reduced the tactical choices of its commanders.

Although the Ethiopian tactics paid handsome dividends during the battle of Adwa, it also meant that the Ethiopian commanders were unable to adapt alternatives in the long haul. For example, the practice of attempting to compensate for the lack of firepower through digging trenches proved to have demoralising effects upon their warriors. For similar reasons, the Ethiopian military was unable to organize and run a systematic insurgency – despite terrain that was highly favourable for guerrilla warfare. Indeed, the latter was something that many of the traditional Ethiopian military elite outright despised. Ras Seyum went on the record to state,

> … a descendant of the Negus Negusti Johannes makes war, but cannot carry on warfare like a shifta (bandit) chief![11]

The final flaw of the traditional Ethiopian military was that while the feudal system allowed for the mobilisation of massive armies, it was very hard to keep all of these deployed in the field for long. Levies especially proved easy to demoralize in the case of repeated defeats.

Probably the greatest weakness of the Ethiopian military of the 1930s was its armament. According to contemporary Italian intelligence reports, it was armed with a motley collection of 400,000 rifles of different origin and type, including decades-old models, but also about 2,000 light- and heavy machine-guns. However, Ethiopians only had 234 artillery pieces, including some captured at Adwa, 40 years previously, and not a few muzzle-loaded bronze cannons. In comparison, the number of modern artillery pieces – such as 20mm Oerlikon anti-aircraft cannons, Stokes mortars, and a few German-made, 37mm PAK-36s – was negligible. Finally, the Ethiopians had a handful of Fiat 3000 light tanks – Renault FT-17s manufactured in Italy under licence – and a few trucks equipped with machine-guns, akin to what are nowadays generally described as 'technicals'. Nevertheless, probably the greatest flaw of the Ethiopian military of the 1930s was that it still had not one factory capable of manufacturing ammunition on a large scale.[12]

Italian Build-Up

Aiming to expand its colonial possessions, in February 1935 Italy announced its intention to invade Ethiopia, and deployed two infantry divisions – the *24th Gavinana* and the *29th Peloritana* – to Italian Somalia. Contrary to earlier Western military expeditions in Africa, the conquest of Ethiopia was not to be attempted on a shoestring: the government of fascist leader Benito Mussolini opted to offer his generals all the means they judged necessary to guarantee a victorious campaign and make a re-edition of the battle of Adwa virtually impossible. Indeed, when General Emilio de Bono, commander of this expedition, requested 100,000 troops for the task, Mussolini responded:

> You will have a 300,000 force, plus 300 to 500 aircraft and 300 fast tanks![13]

Italian logistical preparations were correspondingly massive. The port of Massawa was expanded and a 120-kilometres-long road constructed to Asmara by no less than 30,000 workers. Indeed, by mid-August 1935, a total of 1,700 kilometres of roads had been build and 3,000 kilometres of other roads and tracks refurbished by a true army of no less than 100,000 workers. Furthermore, dozens of wells were dug and numerous depots prepared and filled with massive amounts of supplies necessary to support the invasion.[14] Eventually, at the peak of its involvement in the subsequent invasion, the Italian army deployed as many as 16 divisions in Ethiopia, including two colonial units staffed by Eritreans and six divisions of Black Shirts, as listed in Table 1.

Table 1: Italian Order of Battle in Ethiopia, January 1936 (Main Units)15

Northern Front, Eritrea	
I Army Corps	4th Black Shirts Division 3 Gennaio 5th Alpine Division Pusteria 26th Infantry Division Assietta 30th Infantry Division Sabauda
II Army Corps	3rd Black Shirts Division 21 Aprile 19th Infantry Division Gavinana 24th Infantry Division Gran Sasso
III Army Corps	1st Black Shirt Division 23 Marzo 27th Infantry Division Sila
IV Army Corps	2nd Black Shirts Division 28 Ottobre 5th Black Shirts Division 1 Febbrai 5th Infantry Division Cosseria
Eritrean Army Corps	1st Eritrean Division 2nd Eritrean Division
Southern Front, Somalia	6th Black Shirts Division Tevere 28th Infantry Division Peloritana Infantry Division Libia

In addition to the above divisions, the Italians relied on various semi-regular units, generally designated the 'Dubat', drawn from the local population – especially Somalis. These totalled between 25,000 and 30,000 combatants. Altogether, by 1 October 1935, Italy had massed a force of 161,700 of its own and 53,200 colonial troops in Eritrea, supported by 580 artillery pieces, around 400 light tanks and armoured cars, and 3,700 vehicles. Another 53,850 troops – including 29,500 from regular and semi-regular colonial units, supported by 117 artillery pieces, were present in Somalia. The Italian air force concentrated 132 aircraft in Eritrea and 76 in Somalia: of these, 54 were modern Caproni CA.[101] and Ca.[11] bombers, 83 were Meridionali Ro.[1] reconnaissance aircraft, and 27 were Meridionali Ro.[37] and Fiat CR.[20] fighters.[16]

Slow Fascist Juggernaut

The Italian offensive was opened on 3 October 1935, when multiple units entered Tigray along three primary axes of advance. The I Corps marched from Senafe on Adigrat and Mekelle; the Eritrean Corps advanced from Enticho on Hawzen towards Mekelle, and the II Corps secured the line connecting Adwa – Aksum – Enda Selassie (nowadays Shire). The initial advance encountered no significant resistance, and Adrigat was seized by the next day, followed by Adwa and Axum on 6 and 15 October, respectively. It was only at Adwa that the Italians encountered resistance from a large party of Ethiopian warriors led by Ras Sejjum: this was forced to withdraw when Italians nearly outflanked it. The Ethiopians suffered nearly 400 casualties in this clash, and the Italians 35. During the following days, Haile Selassie Gugsa, an influential noble from Tigray, defected to the Italians in Enticho with his force of 1,200 warriors. Despite the high hopes of the invaders and fierce – indeed notorious – rivalries between the Ethiopian nobility, this remained an exception for the rest of the campaign.

Subsequent Italian advances were significantly slower. The primary reason was not the Ethiopian resistance (this remained relatively light), but the harsh terrain and lack of paved roads which confronted the Italians with ever increasing supply problems. Furthermore, General Emilio de Bono feared a possible Ethiopian counterattack and was thus very cautious. Namely, despite fierce Fascist propaganda about European superiority, the spectre of Adwa remained present in the minds of Italian officers. Eventually,

Italian Black Shirt troops in Mekelle, in mid-December 1935. (NME)

this attracted Mussolini's ire and he quickly replaced de Bono by Marshal Pietro Badoglio. The latter re-launched the advance and captured Mekelle, on 8 November 1935.[17]

In turn, the slow Italian advance enabled a number of Austrian, Cuban, Irish, French, Russian, Swiss, Turkish and US volunteers willing to help, to reach Ethiopia. Some of these were adventurers lacking serious military knowledge, but others were highly experienced officers. The Turkish General Mehmet Wehib Pasha, for example, was former commander of the 2nd Ottoman Army during the Gallipoli campaign, and arrived in company of two further Turkish officers. He was to play an important role during the fighting in the Harar area. Most of US volunteers were of African-American origin and became involved as military advisors and pilots.[18]

Ethiopian Counter-Offensives

By December 1935 the Ethiopians had mobilised their army and began launching their first significant counterattack. Ras Imru and his Army of the Left, in particular, launched the most daring operation of this kind. After assembling his army of 25,000 in Gojjam, they marched for over 960 kilometres (600 miles) to the Shire. Detected by Italian reconnaissance aircraft, Ras Imru's force found itself on the receiving end of attacks from the air. These caused panic among combatants not accustomed to the effects of air power, and nearly half of them deserted. However, those that did not desert quickly learned to decrease effectiveness of air strikes by dispersing and taking cover. Furthermore, their commanders distracted Italians by ordering one group to march in another direction and act as a decoy for enemy aircraft. In that fashion, the Army of the Left managed to outflank the badly overstretched II Army Corps and enter the Shire area.

On 15 December, Ras Imru's 2,000-strong vanguard – led by Fitaurari Shifferaw – crossed the Takezze River after a night march, and then launched an attack on the Dembeguina Pass. This position was held by a battalion-sized colonial unit *Banda Altopiani* under Major Luigi Criniti, reinforced by nine CV.33 tankettes. Shifferaw's men quickly encircled the Italian position and destroyed all of its armoured vehicles. Although Criniti managed a breakthrough, he lost nearly half his troops. Ethiopian losses were also heavy, and included Shifferaw, but the Army of the Left continued its operation and a few days later ambushed a column of Black Shirts underway from Axum, destroying all of its tankettes in the process. Ras Imru then divided his force: while around 8,000 remained in the Af Gaga Pass area, the rest – led by the Ras himself – dashed for Adi Quala in Eritrea, on the other side of the Adi Abo Desert. Their move threatened to cut the II Corp's supply lines and its rear depots.

In an attempt to lessen the threat, the 24th Infantry Division attacked the Af Gaga Pass on 25 December but without success. In desperation, Badoglio authorized the air force to deploy chemical weapons. The first air strike that saw the deployment of mustard gas took place on 22 December 1935. It hit Ras Imru's column with devastating effect. It not only killed dozens, but panicked and demoralized the reminder, prompting them to retreat towards Ende Sellassie, ending this offensive.

From that moment onwards, the Italians made extensive use of the mustard gas, the dreadful effects of which were described by an Ethiopian commander after the II Battle of Tembien as follows:

The bombing from the air had reached its height when suddenly a number of my warriors dropped their weapons, screamed with agony, rubbed their eyes with their knuckles, buckled at the knees and collapsed. An invisible rain of lethal gas was splashing down on my men…I dare not think of how many men I lost on [23 January 1936] alone. The gas contaminated the fields and woods, and at least 2,000 animals died. Mules, cows, rams, and a host of wild creatures, maddened with pain, stampeded to the ravines to throw themselves into the depths below. On the next day, and the next and the next, the Italian aircraft again subjected my army to gas attacks. They dropped it on any spot where they detected the slightest movement.[19]

Similarly, Woreda Kassa, recalled:

They showered mustard gas just like the rain. The poison affected horses, mules and people alike, and by burning up their bodies would finally claim their lives. As a result, the battle became very difficult for us.[20]

Over time the Ethiopians learned to reduce effects of chemical weapons by climbing into hills, above the gas clouds that tended to concentrate low in the valleys. Furthermore, they realized that mustard gas deployed by 105mm artillery shells was less effective than C.500T bombs dropped by Italian bombers: each of the latter contained no less than 220 kilograms of mustard gas apiece.

However, the writing was on the wall when, despite the dubious success of chemical weapons, Badoglio was left without a choice but to request reinforcements from Mussolini. In turn, three additional divisions – the 5th Infantry, the 5th Alpine, and the 26th Infantry – were mobilised and shipped to Eritrea. Their arrival enabled the establishment of the IV Army Corps, in January 1936, which secured Italian bases through occupying and defending the Shire area.

Meanwhile, a column of Black Shirts seized the crucial Warieu Pass, around 30 kilometres from Hawzen – one of the primary entry points into Tigray. The Fascists continued their advance and captured Abbi Addi. On 18 December 1935, around 10,000 Ethiopian warriors counterattacked and forced the Italians to fall back on the pass, but failed to dislodge them from there. During the next few days, both side rushed reinforcements to this sector and this resulted, one month later, in the I Battle of Tembien.

This clash began on 20 January 1936, when the 2nd Black Shirt Division – reinforced by four battalions of Black Shirts – launched an advance on Abbi Addi. Underestimating the strength and resolve of their enemy, the Fascists only stirred a hornet's nest and almost immediately found themselves on the receiving end of fierce counterattacks. By the time they fell back to their starting positions,

Eritrean cavalry advancing into Ethiopia. (National Museum of Ethiopia)

at least two battalions were decimated, and nearly half of the Italian officers were killed. This time, the Ethiopians followed with a general assault on the pass: this nearly broke the back of the 2nd Black Shirt Division. As the Italian commander was preparing to evacuate towards Mekelle, he was reinforced by the 2nd Eritrean Division. A combination of chemical weapons and the counterattack of this unit of 23 January caused massive casualties to the Ethiopians and forced their army to withdraw. By then, the Italians had lost 60 officers, 605 own and 417 Eritrean soldiers killed.[21]

Badoglio's Onslaught
By early February 1936, Italian forces in northern Ethiopia totalled eleven divisions organized into four corps-commands, of which no less than seven were concentrated in the Mekelle sector. It was from there that Marshal Badoglio decided to launch his main blow against Ras Mulugeta's Central Army, half of which was concentrated in the Amba Ardam – a 50 square kilometre plateau and a key feature blocking any advance along the road to Dessie. In preparation for this offensive, the Italians pounded the area with 280 artillery pieces and hundreds of air strikes: their artillerists fired over 1,367 105mm shells filled with mustard gas on Amba Aradam alone.

The onslaught began on 10 February 1936, with assaults by units of the I and III Corps on Amba Aradam in the form of a double encirclement. The Ethiopians reacted by a quick withdrawal and several counterattacks: despite some limited success, the latter proved excessively costly. The Italians thus continued the advance and raised their flag over the plateau's centre on 15 February.

Although suffering devastating losses – not only 8,000 of his warriors fell, but even Ras Mulugeta was killed in an air strike a few days later – thousands of Ethiopian warriors managed to make good their escape because the III Italian Corps was too slow to close the trap in time. Furthermore, the Italians still suffered 802 casualties.[22]

Following the destruction of the Central Army, the Italians turned their attention towards Abbi Addi and launched another two-pronged offensive. At 0100hrs in the morning of 27 February 1936, 60 of their troops stealthily climbed the Worq Amba – a summit dominating this area – took the defenders by surprise, and secured the position. This apparently minor operation opened the way for a general advance of the entire Eritrean Corps in direction of the Warieu Pass. As expected by the Italians, this attack faced fierce counterattacks – up to 14 Ethiopian attempts to recapture Worq Amba were launched – but all of these failed to prevent the battle-hardened colonial troops from reaching Abbi Addi by late in the evening. Further Ethiopian counterattacks – all of them very costly

Italian Caproni Ca.133 bomber, as deployed during invasion of Ethiopia of 1935-1936. (via S. N.)

– were launched against the III Corps: while they prevented the two Italian forces from making their junction on time, the survivors from about 50,000 warriors that were used to defend the area were forced to withdraw between 28 February and 2 March 1936. The Italians later claimed to have killed another 8,000 Ethiopians during the second Tembien Battle, but they again suffered 581 casualties, including 188 Eritrean *Ascaris*.[23]

On 29 February 1936, the two-division strong IV Corps launched an advance over 80 kilometres of desert terrain while the II Corps – including three divisions and an Eritrean brigade – advanced for 25 kilometres along the Adwa-Axum axis. The target of both prongs was Ras Imru's army, now 25,000 strong. As usual, the Ethiopians reacted aggressively. On the same day around 6,000 warriors ambushed the vanguard of the 19th Infantry Division, halting that unit's advance for the next four days. When the Italians resumed their march, they triggered a full-fledged and particularly fierce Ethiopian counterattack – that ended in the by now usual fashion: thousands of warriors cut to pieces by the massively superior firepower of their enemy.

As Ras Imru's decimated units withdrew towards the Takezze River, they were caught by air strikes during which incendiary bombs were deployed for the first time. With his army reduced to a mere few thousands, Ras Imru had no choice but to retreat – this time with the 3rd Eritrean Brigade in hot pursuit. Unsurprisingly, his units disintegrated during the following days, and by mid-March 1936, Ras Imru was left with only a few hundreds of warriors by his side. With this, the most brilliant Ethiopian commander ceased to be a threat for the invaders.[24]

Battle of Maychew

After mopping up the battlefield, the Italians resumed their advance and progressed along the Mekele – Dessie axis with the I Army and the Eritrean Corps. Meanwhile, Emperor Haile Selassie concentrated his remaining forces near the Agumberta Pass, intending to conduct a decisive battle on Saint George's Day, 31 March. Altogether between 55,000 and 65,000 men rallied there, including remnants of the armies defeated at Amba Aradam and Abbi Addi, fresh contingents deployed by Ras Getachew Abate, and the bulk of the Imperial Guard. This last Ethiopian field army was better equipped than its predecessors because it also had about 400 machine guns, at least one battery of 75mm guns, six mortars and several 20mm Oerlikon anti-aircraft cannons.[25]

The Italian radio operators intercepted some of the Ethiopian communications and thus Badoglio was well informed about this concentration in advance. He reacted by positioning six divisions into two defensive lines near the town of Maychew, and left his troops to construct extensive fortifications. His three best divisions protected the first line, with the 5th Alpine on the right, the 2nd

Eritrean in the centre, and the 1st Eritrean on the left. The 30th Infantry, the 4th Black Shirt, and the 26th Infantry divisions covered the flanks and protected the second line. All the commanders were advised not to launch any counterattacks, in order to minimize their own casualties, while imposing attrition upon enemies.

The Ethiopians launched their first assault on the morning of 31 March 1936. Contrary to earlier times their infantry received accurate – even if comparatively limited – artillery support. This silenced one Italian battery and then worked itself methodically over the Italian trenches. By the end of the morning, the assaulters even managed to drive a wedge into the Italians lines and to capture the Mecan Pass. However, soon afterwards, the 2nd Eritrean Division drove them back with a bayonet-charge. Despite staggering losses, continuous and heavy Italian artillery fire, and dozens of air strikes, Haile Selassie ordered another massive assault in the afternoon. This fell apart when a contingent of Oromo cavalry charged into the flank of the Ethiopian infantry instead of the Italians. Despite their numerical and material superiority, the Italians still suffered 1,273 casualties in this battle – including 873 Eritreans. It was their air force that made the difference, and this proved particularly deadly during the subsequent Ethiopian withdrawal: scores of Ethiopian warriors were killed along the shores of the Lake Ascianghi, between 2 and 4 April 1936. The combination of air raids and the harassment of Oromo cavalry actually killed more Ethiopians in these two days than during the Battle of Maychew itself.[26]

Southern Front

The southern front was considered something of a sideshow by both sides in comparison to the campaign waged in the Ethiopian highlands, and the operations there involved lesser forces than deployed on the northern front. Although Marshal Rodolfo Graziani received two metropolitan divisions, he preferred to use colonial forces – foremost the *Libia* Division, and various smaller, regular- and semi-regular units staffed by locals. Largely flat and dry, the Ogaden area in particular favoured mechanized operations and thus Graziani took great care to obtain the necessary vehicles. Eventually, his command totalled only about 500 trucks, 27 armoured cars and 30 CV.33 tanks, but he soon received another 3,300 trucks from Italy, and bought 2,100 trucks and 185 Caterpillar tractors directly from the United States of America (USA).[27]

The Italians opened their invasion by seizing several Ethiopian border posts early during the war, but it was only in November that they launched a multi-battalion advance, supported by tanks and armoured cars, in direction of Gorrahei. The latter was defended by a garrison of about 3,000, including two battalions of the Imperial Guard. However, by the time the Italians reached the town, the Ethiopians dispersed because their leader was killed in an air raid a few days before. The only Italian setback was thus a loss of three tanks to an ambush on 10 November 1935.

Subsequently, the southern front remained relatively quiet, and the Ethiopians – advised by Wehib Pasha, began establishing fortified positions in the Degehaburr area, with intention of defending Harer.[28]

In early December 1935, a force of about 20,000 Ethiopian warriors led by Ras Desta – including two recently established and inexperienced battalions of the Imperial Guards – marched from central Ethiopia towards the south, with the intention of reaching the Somalian town of Dolo. Following a journey of 800 kilometres (nearly 500 miles), they reached the confines of the border between Ethiopia, Kenya and Somalia in early 1936. On 6 January that year, Ras Desta's force established several camps in the Juba Valley,

Pilots and ground crews of the Royal Italian Air Force around one of heavier bombs deployed during the Abyssinian Campaign of 1936. (Wikimedia Commons)

Wehib Pasha with his two adjutants in Ethiopia. (Wikimedia Commons)

around 100 kilometres (62 miles) short of Dolo. It was there that they were detected by reconnaissance aircraft of the Italian air force – and promptly subjected to repeated bombing.

Alerted, Graziani concentrated a force of 14,000 men, supported by 26 artillery pieces, dozens of armoured vehicles, and about 700 trucks, in the Dolo area. Having everything in place, and following extensive air raids by up to 50 bombers on Ethiopian camps, on 13 January he launched a three-pronged advance. Ras Desta's force was not only caught by surprise, but then outmanoeuvred too, because the flat terrain along the Juba River proved ideal for rapidly moving Italian armour. After suffering a loss of about 3,000 men, they withdrew into the Wadrara forest, and began constructing a defensive line.

Meanwhile, Graziani contended himself with the elimination of a threat and decided not to press any further. Nevertheless, the battle was still not over when, on 16 January, 904 Eritrean soldiers of the IV Brigade of the *Libia* Division deserted and ran over the border to Kenya. Possibly caused by religious motives – because many of the Eritreans in question were Christians, who had to fight against Ethiopian Christians while assigned to a division largely consisting of Moslems – this case remained an exception.[29]

Over the next two months, the Italians were not only delayed by heavy rainfalls, but were also building-up a concentration of 38,000 troops for attack on Harer. Proceeded by General Nasi's *Libia* Division, this offensive was launched on 13 April 1936, but almost immediately subjected to a strong counterattack by a force of 10,000 Ethiopian warriors under Dejaz Abebe and Dejaz Makonnen. Launched in the Danan area, this assault was actually designed to pre-empt the Italian offensive, but came late. After three days of fighting, the Ethiopians were forced to withdraw due to the threat of being outflanked by motorized enemy units. On 24 and 25 April 1936, the Italians assaulted the fortified line in the Degehabur area

and – contrary to Wehib Pasha's expectations – easily overwhelmed them. Indeed, Dagehabur was captured on 30 April, despite several Ethiopian counterattacks.[30]

The Fall of Addis Ababa

The defeats of Maychew and Degehabur proved decisive and enabled the Italians a rapid advance on all fronts. The Eritrea Brigade – which had been sent to pursuit the remnants of Ras Imru's army – reached the Gondar area in late March, but then had to stop in order to wait for a 3,400-strong motorized column under Fascist hierarch Achille Starace, which advanced separately. With the Italian propaganda insisting on the place being taken by a fascist force, Gondar was thus invested only from 1 April 1936. Starace's column then advanced on Debra Tabor, and captured this town on 28 April 1936. Meanwhile, the Eritrean Brigade progressed along the shores of the Lake Tana, before capturing Bahir Dar.[31]

Elsewhere, the I Corps seized Dessie in mid-April, and Badoglio then opened preparations for the final advance of 400 kilometres (250 miles) on Addis Ababa. The last phase of the Italian invasion thus began on 24 April 1936, when the 30th Infantry Division – motorized for this operation and baptised the *Colona de ferrea volonta* ('Iron Will Column') – left Dessie. With its flanks secured by infantry units – foremost one of the Eritrean brigades – the 30th advanced with ease, because Ethiopian commanders proved unable to organize the defence of their capital. Indeed, the 'last ditch defence' was put up only by cadets of the Holeta Military School. Addis Ababa fell on 5 May 1936, and three days later Emperor Selassie fled by train to Djibouti.

In the south, Graziani's forces took Jijjiga on 6 May, and Harer two days later, before joining Badoglio's troops at Dire Dawa on 10 May 1936.[32]

Selassie's Return

The fall of Addis Ababa and the exile of the Emperor did not end the war. Several Ethiopian armies remained in the field, determined to offer resistance. This became obvious on 28 July, when they

Eritrean Ascaris advancing into the desert of Ogaden. (Wikimedia Commons)

Advance of Italian tankettes in Ethiopia. (Wikimedia Commons)

Emperor Selassie testing a French-made Hotchkiss M1914 machine gun. (Wikimedia Commons)

attempted to infiltrate and assault the capital, but were easily repulsed by the Italian garrison. Following the end of the rainy season, in October 1936, the Italians thus launched multiple expeditions to hunt down the remaining Ethiopian forces. On 18 December 1936, Ras Imru was cornered and forced to surrender, while the last battle of the war took place on 19 February 1937, when the remnants of Ras Desta's army were beaten, although the injured Ras managed to avoid capture and escape.[33]

Thousands of other Ethiopian warriors escaped and rallied around remaining commanders, willing to continue the struggle. Later colloquially known as the 'Patriots', they continued to fight despite the lack of any kind of support – until the Italian defeat of 1941.

Far from ending the conflict, the fall of Addis Ababa in May 1936 merely offered the Italians an opportunity to make mistakes that virtually guaranteed that their rule would never be accepted by Ethiopians. On 19 February 1937, two Patriots managed to throw several hand-grenades at Italian officials during a celebration in front of the former Imperial Palace in Addis Ababa, injuring Graziani and several others.

This attack triggered large-scale reprisals against civilians: at least 30,000 were summarily executed by the Carabinieri, Black Shirts and Italian colonists over the next three days in what became known as 'Yekatit 12' (19 February). Furthermore, dozens of suspects were detained, tried and executed in the following weeks.

To add salt to the injury, three months later Italians arrested and executed 297 monks of the Debre Libanos Monastery – one of holiest places in Ethiopia. As a result, the number of Patriots increased dramatically, and insurgents became active in nearly all of the country.

In March and April 1938, the Italians were forced to launch a large-scale operation – including 60,000 troops – to re-establish their control over Gojjam, but such ventures had short-terms effects only, due to several factors. Foremost was that the Patriots remained completely disunited and continued operating in dispersed groups; another was that the Ethiopians eventually did opt for guerrilla tactics, and avoided engagements with superior enemy forces. While this meant that the Patriots were unable to capture any of the areas held by the invaders, it resulted in a stalemate, which the Italians could not afford: most of the countryside was controlled by local insurgent groups, while all the towns were in Italian hands – and all the vehicles travelling from one place to the other had to do so in well-protected convoys.[34]

Eventually, the Italian occupation proved short-lived. Only few months after Italy's entry into the World War II, the British had concentrated enough forces in Sudan and Kenya to launch an offensive against Rome's isolated possessions in Eastern Africa. On 19 January 1941, two British divisions entered Eritrea and defeated the Italians at Keren in a long and bloody battle, before securing Asmara, on 1 April.

Meanwhile, another force advanced from Kenya into Somalia, starting with 24 January, then captured Mogadishu and Harer, before reaching Addis Ababa on 6 April 1941. Last but not least, a small composite detachment under the famous Orde Wingate – including not just British, but also Sudanese and Ethiopian troops trained by the British, and accompanied by Emperor Haile Selassie – entered Ethiopia on 20 January 1941. Named 'Gideon Force', this unit liberated the towns of Burye, on 4 March, and Debra Markos, on 3 April, by successfully outflanking and bluffing far larger Italian units. Gideon Force then set straight for the capital, reaching it on 5 May 1941, when the Emperor made a triumphal return.[35]

CHAPTER 2
FROM THE NEGUS TO THE DERG

One of the most pressing tasks for Emperor Selassie upon his return was to rebuild a military and reinstate a measure of governmental control over the country that was meanwhile in complete disorder. Initially, he had no other choice but to request support of the British, and they agreed to help train and arm a force of ten infantry battalions, one artillery regiment, a small regiment equipped with armoured cars, and some engineers and signallers. The British Military Mission to Ethiopia (BMME) was created to run this operation, and a British officer appointed to each of the emerging battalions, while a number of young Ethiopians underwent training at the Royal Military College. Thus came into being a nucleus of the new Ethiopian military. This was involved in combat operations before long.[36]

Uprising in Eastern Tigray
The process of reasserting Selassie's rule over all of Ethiopia was to prove very difficult, especially in Tigray. Attempts to raise taxes by local officials – many of whom were corrupt – repeatedly triggered dissatisfaction in the local peasantry. Nobility began openly disagreeing with Addis Ababa's attempts to impose centralized authority. Flushed with arms left behind by the Italians, and full of former Patriots, the province became a highly insecure area.[37]

After three British officers and nine Ethiopian troops were killed in an ambush on 11 January 1942, Selassie deployed up to 35,000 troops under the command of the Crown Prince and Ras Seyum. While this massive operation did re-establish some semblance of government control, it also antagonized the local peasantry, who had to keep the troops supplied with food, while armed bands continued roaming the countryside. In May 1942, an army unit deployed to suppress cattle-stealing was ambushed and routed near Ambalage. This action triggered a large-scale uprising in the entire region, resulting in thousands of bandits, peasants and nobles gathering in the Maychew area, where they rallied around Haile Mariam Redda.[38]

The emerging insurgent movement first put the garrison of Quiha under siege, and then assaulted it on 17 September 1943. The defenders were overrun after a six-hour battle. The next day,

Official photograph of Emperor Selassie from the late 1960s. (Albert Grandolini Collection)

the insurgents took the Fort Enda Yesus, and then Mekelle, the provincial capital.

After this victory, Heile Mariam Redda's army advanced on the Amba Alagi Pass. However, Addis Ababa meanwhile deployed reinforcements to Tigray, including 34 BMME officers under the command of Ras Abebe Aregai, and the newly-established 5th

One of two de Havilland D. H.60 Tiger Moths acquired by Ethiopia in 1945, and used for basic training at the flight school in Harar Meda. (Pit Weinert Collection)

During the so-called 'Swedish period', Ethiopian Air Force acquired 16 SAAB B.17 dive-bombers, starting in late 1947. The type remained in service until 1977. (Pit Weinert Collection)

Except for US-made aircraft, Ethiopia also acquired 15 M8 Greyhound 6x6 light armoured cars, armed with 37mm cannons and two machine guns, in 1955; 15 in 1956 and 15 of the M20 variant in 1959. (Albert Grandolini Collection)

Battalion. Starting on 18 September 1943, the insurgents repeatedly attacked army positions on Amba Alagi, using the traditional pattern of encirclement and large-scale infantry assaults, but the well-trained regulars held their ground – impressing their British advisors with their discipline and steadiness. Indeed, Redda's combatants suffered dreadful casualties, and then came under attack by Bristol Blenheim Bombers of the Royal Air Force (RAF).

While the newly-established IEAF was re-equipped with aircraft of Swedish origin, the Ethiopian Army obtained CKD AH IVb light tanks of Czechoslovak manufacture, armed with two Skoda 7,92mm machine guns. Ordered in June 1948 and delivered by ship to Djibouti, and then by rail to Addis Ababa in 1950, these vehicles with crew of two remained in service until the early 1980s, and at least a company of them saw combat service during the Ogaden War. (Albert Grandolini Collection)

Redda regrouped his forces and repeated the assault in early October, but was beaten back with heavy losses once again. Already weakened by tensions among its top commanders, his army subsequently dispersed, thus ending the revolt. Nevertheless, the Ethiopian military then launched a campaign of brutal mop-up operations in eastern Tigray, destroying numerous villages in the process.[39]

US Aid

Although Great Britain helped rebuild the Imperial Ethiopian Army (IEA), Haile Selassie always complained about the British lack of interest in supporting him. To a certain degree this was ·correct, because London was only ready to help establish an Ethiopian military that would not become a potential threat to its colonies in the neighbourhood. Correspondingly, most of the weapons supplied by the British to the Ethiopians were from captured Italian stocks, and often very highly priced. Despite continuous negotiations and increasing pressure, London also refused to help build up an air force. Eventually, this resulted in growing tensions and the British were requested to leave in 1951. Once again Addis Ababa turned to other sources of aid.[40]

A Swedish military advisory team returned in 1941, and helped re-open the Holeta Military School. Furthermore, during the late 1940s and early 1950s, the Swedes provided substantial assistance in establishment of the Imperial Ethiopian Air Force (IEAF). However, most important for the further development of the Ethiopian military became cooperation with the USA, opened on 22 May 1953 through the signing of an Ethiopian-American Mutual Defence Agreement. Set for 25 years, this treaty included the lease of the Kagnew radio station to the US military: this strategic facility was crucially important for relaying communications between the Middle East and the Far East. In return, Washington agreed to deploy a Military Assistance Advisory Group (MAAG) to Ethiopia and help train the army and the air force.[41]

On US advice, the existing military was re-organized as detailed in the Table 2, and included various support units – between them one armoured squadron, one engineering battalion, and one artillery regiment. As such, the army totalled 21,980 men in 1956. By this time, the IEA included a small military intelligence section initially staffed by US and Israeli personnel.[42]

Training of Ethiopian bazooka operators under the watchful eyes of US instructors, in the late 1950s. (Albert Grandolini Collection)

US-donated M101 light howitzers represented heaviest artillery pieces in Ethiopian arsenal of the 1960s. (Albert Grandolini Collection)

Table 2: Imperial Ethiopian Army Order of Battle, 1956[43]

Unit	HQ	Sub-Units	Manpower
1st Division	Addis Ababa	1st, 2nd, 3rd Brigades	5,385
2nd Division	Asmara	5th, 6th, 7th, 8th, 12th Brigades	4,557
3rd Division	Harer	4th, 9th, 10th, 11th Brigades	6,890

Furthermore, in 1958, the Territorial Army – created back in 1941 to integrate various bands of insurgents that fought against Italians – was significantly reorganized. Men enrolled to serve with this auxiliary force were trained for three months and then recalled for two further months of service every year.

Somali Threat

As described in detail in Volume 18 of this series, the US military aid proved highly important for further development of the Imperial Ethiopian Air Force too. During the late 1950s, an increasing number of IEAF personnel were trained by American advisors, and the service gradually re-equipped with a total of 14 Douglas C-47 and 2 Douglas C-54 transports (deliveries began in 1956), 18 North American T-28A trainers (delivered between 1958 and 1962), 14 Lockheed T-33A jet trainers (deliveries began in 1957), and 28 North American F-86F Sabre jet fighters (delivered between 1960

Another US-donated artillery piece in service with the Ethiopian Army since the 1960s was the 75mm M116 pack howitzer. Mass produced, it was custom tailored for movement across difficult terrain. (Albert Grandolini Collection)

and 1970).[44]

Despite US and Swedish aid, and although Addis Ababa was spending at least a third of its annual budget for defence-related purposes, overall growth of the Ethiopian military remained relatively slow. Even as of 1960, the IEA was considered by its US advisors as unable to fight a well-equipped army and principally adapted for internal security tasks.[45] One of the reasons is that for most of the late 1950s Ethiopian military commanders emphasised quality upon quantity. Correspondingly, local military educational facilities not only accepted only the best and fittest candidates, but actually decreased their output of new officers to a level where only between five and ten were graduating from different colleges annually.

The situation began to change following the independence of Sudan, but especially that of Somalia – where already the first government declared its commitment to unify all the Somalis, and thus annex the Ethiopian province of Ogaden. Frustrated by the limited aid provided by Western powers, Somalia turned to the Union of Soviet Socialist Republics (USSR or Soviet Union) and signed a contract worth US$ 30 million in October 1963, which included large orders for enough arms to expand its military from 4,000 to 20,000, including a well-equipped air force.

Already shaken by a coup attempt by the Swedish-trained Imperial Body Guard in December 1960, and also at the first signs of a nascent insurgency in Eritrea, Emperor Heile Selassie requested an increase in US military aid, sometimes exaggerating the Somali threat – as and if necessary. Washington reacted positively, despite earlier reservations that a further build-up would result in a military that the Ethiopian economy was ill-positioned to support in the long turn. Correspondingly, the amount granted to Addis Ababa by the Pentagon increased from US$5 million a year in 1961, to more than US$10 million in 1974.[46]

This enabled the next phase of expansion of the IEA and the IEAF. All the units of the prestigious 3rd 'Lion' Division in Ogaden were motorized, and this unit was reinforced through the addition of a tank battalion equipped with 54 US-made M41 Walker Bulldog light tanks. Similarly the 4th Division was activated to guard southern Ethiopia, while the air force received a squadron-worth of 12 Northrop F-5A and 2 F-5B Freedom Fighter jets, all pilots for which were trained in the USA. While deliveries and working-up of the IEAF's first F-5-unit were to last for several years longer, by 1966, the IEA's total manpower had grown to 38,000: the force

Staff and cadets of the IEAF's Flight School at Debre Zeit, late 1960s. A total of 48 SAAB 91 Safir basic trainers were acquired by Ethiopia in the 1960s, and they provided good service until 1973. (Pit Weinert Collection)

A total of 28 F-86F Sabre fighter jets from surplus US stocks represented the mainstay of the IEAF's fighter force in the 1960s. This example was photographed during their temporary deployment to the Democratic Republic of the Congo, within the framework of a UN peace-keeping mission in 1961. (Pit Weinert Collection)

One of 14 C-47 transports donated to the IEAF starting in 1956. Notable is that they wore the full service title – in Amharic and in English – applied in black below the cockpit. (Albert Grandolini Collection)

not only included an airborne brigade, but also received 39 M75 armoured personnel carriers (APCs) from surplus US stocks.[47]

Finally, by 1974, the IEA received its first batch of 11 M60 main battle tanks (MBTs), over 100 M113 APCs, and was in the process of building up an aviation branch equipped with – amongst others – 16 Bell UH-1H Huey helicopters donated by the USA. Similarly, the IEAF was reinforced through the acquisition of four English Electric Canberra bombers, and then placed an order for delivery of 16 Northrop F-5E Tiger II fighter jets, AIM-9 Sidewinder guided air-to-air missiles, and two Westinghouse AN/TPS-43D long range early warning radars. Still totalling about 37,700 – of whom several hundreds were always undergoing various training courses in the USA – the Ethiopian military of 1974 was considered well-organized, well-trained, and far superior to the armies of any of neighbouring countries, although primarily composed of infantry units and including only five artillery-, two tank-, four mechanized- and motorized, and two engineer battalions.[48]

Ethiopian Revolution

For a large number of reasons – including the Emperor's authoritarian grip on power, fierce competition amongst factions in the governmental elites, increasing social tensions due to the limited modernisation of the country's economic structures – unrest began to spread through Ethiopia in the 1960s. However, it was only the draught of the early 1970s that such factors as food scarcity in some provinces, and student protests really undermined the throne. When, because of the rise of oil prices on the international markets, the government decreed a doubling of the oil prices, taxi drivers went on strike and were quickly joined by public teachers and radical students. As the government failed to act decisively, bigger and bigger manifestations took place in the streets of Addis Ababa.[49]

The waves of discontent would probably not have been enough to end the thousand year-old Solomonic dynasty without the large scale mutinies that erupted at the same time in the armed forces. The IEA in particular was socially divided because most of the soldiers and NCOs were of rural or poor urban background, while the subaltern officers educated at the Holeta Military Academy were generally of middle-class background, whereas top officers, trained in the more prestigious Harar Military Academy, were mostly from well-off families or the aristocracy.[50]

Motivated by dissatisfaction over living conditions, the first mutinies erupted in mid-January 1974 in the 4th Territorial Army Brigade (the Territorial Army was subsequently re-organized into the People's Militia), and were initially small-scale affairs. They quickly spread out of control: the entire 2nd Division mutinied on 25 February, followed by the 4th Division and then the 3rd, which mutinied between 7 and 13 April 1974. Most of the mutineers elected deputies – almost exclusively drawn from the ranks of middle officers: on 27 June 1974, these constituted the 109-member-

Mengistu Heile Mariam during a speech in Addis Ababa of 1977. He established himself in charge of the Derg and then in control of Ethiopia in the course of three years of murderous power struggle in which thousands were executed or disappeared. (Albert Grandolini Collection)

strong Coordinating Committee of the Armed Forces, Police, and Territorial Army. This became a de-facto political body, standing in competition with the throne.[51]

The power balance shifted decisively when 200 members of the administration and the aristocracy were arrested on 26 April 1974, proving further that Haile Selassie had become powerless. Finally, the Emperor was deposed – and executed secretly soon afterwards – and thus the monarchy abolished, on 12 September 1974. Three days later, the Armed Forces Committee became the Provisional Military Administrative Council (PMAC), universally known as the 'Derg' ('Committee' in Amharic). The Derg established itself as the supreme political organ of the country.[52]

Although facing fierce internal rivalries, a young officer of the 3rd Division, Mengistu Haile Mariam (promoted to the rank of Colonel only in November 1976), eventually manoeuvred himself towards the top of the Derg while ruthlessly eliminating all of his rivals. The first president of the PMAC, Major General Mikael Andom was killed on 23 November 1974, while Mengistu's last serious competitor – Lieutenant Colonel Atnafu Abata – was executed together with 40 other officers on 13 November 1977. By the end of the same year, Mengistu's hold on power was uncontested.[53]

While the air force largely kept itself out of political affairs, the army was heavily involved. Because the struggle for power was not limited to the Derg, the officer corps of the former IEA was literally decimated by successive waves of purges. Furthermore, the Derg began a merciless struggle against several competing civilian factions – often despite their grossly similar political lines. While the leftist Pan-Ethiopian Socialist Movement opted not to use violence against the new government, the Ethiopian People's Revolutionary Party

– created in 1975 – made the opposite choice and began launching attacks in the capital. The Derg reacted by unleashing a protracted campaign of repression – tellingly named the 'Red Terror' – which resulted in the disappearance and summary executions of thousands of real or perceived opponents. By the end of 1977, the People's Revolutionary Party was not only unable to strike on the capital, but almost completely destroyed.[54]

Problems Everywhere

The chaos in Addis Ababa and in the army had devastating effects upon the stability of the whole of Ethiopia. The government of neighbouring Somalia in particular lost no time in exploiting the situation. The country has already lost one short war against Ethiopia, in 1964, when the IEA quickly chased away the main Somali Army concentration from Ethiopian soil.[55]

Over the following ten years, successive Somali governments had to acknowledge that even the Soviet aid was insufficient to match the Ethiopian military power: Mogadishu was heavily dependent on donations from abroad – only a few of which ever materialized. Correspondingly, while insurgents of the Western Somali Liberation Front (WSLF, sometimes called the United Liberation Front of Western Somalia) remained active inside Ethiopia – and eventually brought up to 124,000 square kilometres of the Bale province under their control in 1965 – their success remained limited, because Somalia proved unable to support them. Indeed, when General Wolde Selassie Bereka had been named Governor of Bale Province in 1968, he immediately launched a cohesive counter-insurgency (COIN) campaign. While quickly sacking all of the corrupt officials and reshuffling the local administration, he deployed two brigades of the 3rd Division – supported by the local militias, police, and units of the Territorial Army – to cut off opposition from Somalia. Divided along clan lines, the insurgents proved unable to resist: between February and March 1970, their two most important leaders surrendered, and thus Ethiopia re-asserted its control over most of the Bale province once again.[56]

However, once Emperor Selassie was overthrown, and as the different factions in the Ethiopian capital continued tearing each other apart in the mid-1970s, the Somali government – since 1969 dominated by Major-General Siad Barre – reinforced its support for Somali irredentists. Barre's government re-launched its support for the WSLF and this brought most of rural Ogaden under its control by early 1976. Because Mogadishu never managed to establish firm control over this group, and after his negotiations with Addis Ababa over regional autonomy of Ogaden failed, the Somali strongman then ordered his military to establish another insurgent group, the Somali-Abo Liberation Front (SALF). While originally led by few WSLF-veterans, the SALF functioned as a proxy of the government in Mogadishu and was largely staffed by Somali Army officers. Facing two insurgencies supported by most of the local population, what was left of the Ethiopian Army in Ogaden was soon confined to its bases. The Ethiopian Minister of Defence estimated that in July 1977, the two movements included as many as 39,450 combatants. During the same month, Barre unleashed his military into an undeclared invasion of Ethiopia. Only slowly recognized by the Derg, this action resulted in the conflict known as the Ogaden War, during the first phase of which the Somalis brought most of the Ethiopian province, including the town of Gode, under their control and were stopped only in Dire Dawa and short of Harer.[57]

Meanwhile, a new uprising erupted in Tigray in 1975, where the Tigrayan People's Liberation Front (TPLF) became active. Finally, the disorganisation of the Ethiopian armed forces had far reaching consequences in so far that the local insurgency – that in Eritrea which was ongoing since 1961 (see the following chapter) – brought most of that province under its control. During the summer and autumn of 1977, Ethiopia was thus facing multiple and massive threats to its integrity and sovereignty.

CHAPTER 3
THE DERG NEMESIS

The wars that devastated Ethiopia and Eritrea between the mid-1970s and 1991, saw the involvement of a host of different armed movements. Although these tied down large parts of the military, most of them never developed into a major threat to the central government: the centrepiece of the military conflict became the struggle between three major protagonists: the Derg on one side, the biggest insurgent movement in Eritrea, and another one in Tigray.

Eritrean Insurgency

Colonised by the Italians in 1882, and occupied by the British since 1941, Eritrea came under a UN mandate in 1950, because the Soviet Union stunned Western Allies by requesting trusteeship over that area during the Potsdam Conference in 1945. After British withdrawal, Eritrea came under full Ethiopian control, and Emperor Selassie gradually reduced Eritrean autonomy and local democratic institutions. In 1955, he federated the area to become one of nine provinces making up the Ethiopian union, and officially annexed it in 1962, submitting all decision-making to dictate from Addis Ababa.

Not all Eritreans found this decision acceptable: strikes and public demonstrations erupted in 1958, and a pro-independence group – the Eritrean Liberation Movement (ELM) – was founded in Sudan. In July 1960, another organization, the Eritrean Liberation Front (ELF), was formed in Cairo by Muslim lowlanders who gathered around Hamid Idris Awate (or Adam). The ELF gained limited support from Syria after the Ba'athist take-over in March 1963, and later from Iraq and Libya – both of which perceived this group as 'pro-Arab' (because of its predominantly Muslim leadership, and because of Israel's support for Ethiopia). However, Awate never managed to overcome countless issues of ethnicity, clans and ideology between his followers. Furthermore, the ELF found it hard to draw support outside the lowland areas (dominated by Muslims) and its insurgency, initiated in 1961, remained rather limited in scope and success for most of the following years.[58]

The ELF's military wing – the Eritrean Liberation Army (ELA) – was led by Idris Osman Galewdewos, but its beginnings were rather modest. Originally, it included just a small group of insurgents from the Bani Amir tribe, active in western Eritrea. During subsequent years, they were reinforced by 30 deserters from the police that took their firearms and ammunition with them, and about 80 former soldiers of the Sudanese army. As of 1963, the ELA's strength was still limited to about 250 combatants, and by 1966 it had increased to only about 500, although the group slowly began to increase the frequency of its operations with some help from Khartoum: the number of its attacks increased from four in 1962, to 21 in 1964, and 27 in 1966.[59]

Meanwhile, the ELA was reorganized into four, and then five, zones along the pattern previously used by the National Liberation Front in Algeria. Each of these was led by a local commander who quickly became quite independent from the top leadership that

The ELA operated in very small groups of poorly armed, but highly motivated, insurgents for most of the 1960s. Most of them wore civilian clothes and were armed with obsolete firearms. (Albert Grandolini Collection)

remained abroad. Despite their common purpose, and a centralized training structure, ELA's units from different zones thus rarely cooperated. Their organization as of 1966 was as provided in Table 3.

Table 3: ELA Zones, 1966[60]

Designation	Operational Area	Commander
1st Zone	Border to Sudan	Mahmud Dinai
2nd Zone	Keren	Umar Aziz
3rd Zone	Northern Sahel	Abd al-Karim Ahmad
4th Zone	Massawa	Mugammad Ali Umaru
5th Zone	Asmara & Central Highlands	Wolde Kashai

The initial Ethiopian response to the ELA was restrained, and limited to the deployment of dedicated units of the Imperial Ethiopian Police – the 'Fetno Derash' (Emergency Police, also known as the Commando Police). On the contrary, the IEA not only did not increase its presence, but kept only one brigade of the 2nd Division deployed in all of Eritrea. One of its battalions was based in Keren, another in Asmara, and the third along the road connecting Massawa with Asmara. Originally trained in riot control, the Fetno

Insurgents of the ELA seen while being briefed by their commander in the late 1960s. (Albert Grandolini Collection)

Two soldiers of the 2nd Division of the Imperial Ethiopian Army in Eritrea of the late 1960s. (Albert Grandolini Collection)

Derash was gradually expanded and re-trained by Israeli advisors until it totalled about 7,000 well-trained police-officers and became a dedicated COIN asset.[61]

The situation in Eritrea thus began seriously deteriorating only in early 1967 when the IEA felt prompted to re-deploy the 25th and 33rd brigades of the 2nd Division to this province, and then launched a three-phased operation codenamed Wegaw ('Trash'). This attempt to suppress the ELF in western Eritrea resulted in the arrest of anybody suspected of collaboration with, or support of, insurgents and destruction of their property – which in turn forced thousands of civilians to flee their homes.[62]

During the following years, the IEA continued to launch periodic brigade-sized operations. Simultaneously, it established a network of company- and battalion-sized positions to control crucial locations. Although still often praised even by well-informed Ethiopians, this effort was compromised by a number of flaws. While the units involved were launching frequent patrols into their area of responsibility, they did this generally in company-sized formations – which proved easy to avoid for small groups of insurgents. Furthermore, the Ethiopians failed to establish a functional joint headquarters (HQ) that could coordinate all the activities of the IEA, the Fetno Derash and the Territorial Army, while the HQ of the 2nd Division had no quick reaction force. Furthermore, the support of the IEAF remained limited to two or three helicopters: the 2nd Group of the air force – responsible for providing air support to army units in Eritrea – failed to provide forward air controllers (FACs), while army FACs lacked adequate radio equipment.[63]

Air Force to the Rescue

Overall, while actually designed and regularly trained to fight COIN warfare, the governmental bodies failed to prevent the expansion of the insurgency, although they retained effective control over all of the towns, cities and major land communications. That said, the insurgency remained plagued by disunity, in 1965, ELM fighters attacked a party of the ELM when this attempted to enter Eritrea while coming from Sudan.

A far more serious crisis erupted a few years later when newly-recruited fighters began to challenge the policies of the ELF's original leadership. Namely, a group of 35 volunteers who underwent training in China and felt defrauded by the British, the UN, and the Ethiopians, began openly criticising the ELA's division into zones, and advocating a reorganization of the movement along the patterns of the Mao Tse Dong's doctrine of 'People's War'. Before long internal debates degenerated into a wave of assassinations and despite some reconciliation attempts, three distinct groups split from the ELA in 1970.[64]

During that year, the Ethiopian authorities finally realized the seriousness of the situation and the IEAF was ordered to deploy around a dozen old SAAB B.17 fighter-bombers to Asmara. In response to several air strikes, the ELA launched a campaign of assassinations of top officers, and – amongst others – ambushed and killed the commanding officer (CO) of the 2nd Infantry Division, General Teshome Ergete, on 21 November 1970. While the army reacted by re-deploying reinforcements to Eritrea and neighbouring Tigray, the IEAF sent two Canberra bombers and at least two F-86F Sabres to Asmara airfield. These were soon sighted flying air strikes against selected targets – and deploying napalm bombs in abundance. Furthermore, the IEAF established the 3rd Squadron, equipped with eight T-28As – all of which were upgraded to T-28D Trojan standard before delivery from the USA – as its specialized COIN outfit. Through its existence, this unit benefited immensely from cooperation with the US MAAG team, many members of which completed at least one tour of duty in Vietnam. The 3rd Squadron was deployed at Asmara in 1971, by which time it was reinforced with several SAAB B.17s.[65]

Under pressure, but also on impulse of such former Chinese trainees like Issayas Afeworki and Ramadan Muhammad Nur, the three splinter groups of the ELA re-aligned and partially merged in October 1972 – although it was only in 1977, during the tenure of a Congress – that the Eritrean People's Liberation Front (EPLF) was formally created. Indeed, the ELF did not favour the emergence

Emperor Selassie inspecting aircraft, pilots and ground crews of the newly-established 3rd Squadron, a specialized COIN unit, in the early 1970s. Notable is one of eight T-28D of this squadron in the background right: left in bare metal overall, it was armed with a gun-pod with a Browning M2 machine gun. (Pit Weinert Collection)

In addition to T-28s, the 3rd Squadron also flew a handful of SAAB B.17 dive-bombers, one of which is seen in this photograph from the late 1960s, together with pilots and Emperor Selassie. Notable is the huge national insignia under the right wing of this aircraft. (Pit Weinert Collection)

As the intensity of insurgent operations in Eritrea increased, in the early 1970s, the IEAF began forward deploying its F-86F Sabres to airports in Asmara and Massawa. This example – the serial number of which was deleted by censor – was photographed while equipped with hardpoints for launch rails for 2.75in (68mm) unguided rockets. (EtAF via S. N.)

The EPLF came into being through merger of three splinter factions of the ELF/ELA, in 1977. Although its 'I Congress', held in 1977, was held under most primitive conditions, it had far-reaching consequences. (Albert Grandolini Collection)

of competition and the ELA began attacking its rivals even before their unification in February 1972 – triggering a civil war among insurgents that lasted until November 1974.[66]

Meanwhile, the increased activity of the IEAF prompted the insurgents to launch their first claims for Ethiopian aircraft supposedly shot down in combat. By 1975, no less than seven aircraft were claimed to have been brought down by ground fire, including two F-86s. However, it seems that only one of IEAF's Trojans was actually written off – and then to other causes. The operational standards and combat efficiency of IEAF pilots remained exceptionally high, but the T-28s began suffering engine-related problems caused by intensive flying. Indeed, the 3rd COIN Squadron is known to have been left with only 6 operational Trojans and fewer than 10 SAABs by 1974.[67]

Bloody Stalemate

The coup against Emperor Selassie and the subsequent period of power struggle in Addis Ababa resulted in a temporary disorganisation and disengagement of the Ethiopian military in Eritrea – even more so because the two main Eritrean movements

ceased fighting each other in November 1974. Under increasing pressure, the army reduced the number of garrisons from 60 to 17 by early 1975, and controlled only Masawa, Asmara and a few isolated towns. Emboldened, the ELF launched a series of guerrilla attacks on Asmara; while failing to dislodge the garrison these prompted the military into the repression of the local population, which in turn caused numerous volunteers to rally the EPLF and the ELF. Furthermore, purges in the army also targeted soldiers and officers of Eritrean origin and significant numbers of them defected to the insurgents – who in turn benefitted from the excellent training and experience of these new recruits.[68]

Reinforced, the ELF and the EPLF began establishing larger units and launching ever larger operations. On 31 January 1975, they opened a joint assault on Asmara. Although this was repulsed after a 10-day long battle, 110 similar operations were undertaken elsewhere during the rest of the year, 15 of which were coordinated between two organizations. In the course of these the insurgents captured enough arms, fuel, other equipment and vehicles that the ELF began using trucks instead of camels and mules.[69]

Facing a new situation, the Derg declared a State of Emergency in Eritrea in February 1975, and then opted to create a new, dedicated COIN force, separated from the conventional army: the 'Neblebal' ('Flame'). Officers and other ranks for this organization were drawn from the regular army – including its elite Airborne Brigade – to form ten 400-man strong battalions numbered from 201 to 210. They were then sent to four different camps for eight months of intensive training by Israeli instructors. Once operational, nine of these units were deployed in Eritrea where they played a significant role in repulsing further insurgent assaults into urban areas, although proving far too few to change the overall situation. In early 1976, they were involved in the first major COIN operation launched by the Derg, code-named Raza ('Vulture'). This included the mobilisation of up to 100,000 peasants that were levied in Tigray, Gondar, Gojjam and Wello provinces, and an attempt to overwhelm the insurgents by the sheer weight of numbers. However, because only 40,000 of involved combatants have received any kind of serious military training – and then only two weeks of the same, and even they were armed with obsolete weapons – this enterprise proved anything but successful. Organized into five columns commanded by Lieutenant-Colonel Getahun Tekle Mariam, they were ambushed even before entering Eritrea in May 1975, and suffered hundreds of casualties, while about 600 were taken prisoners. Worst of all, because this expedition was devoid of logistical support, hundreds died of thirst and starvation during the subsequent retreat.

Nevertheless, the experience with deploying the Neblebal units proved a success, and thus a second batch of ten battalions – numbered 211 to 220 – was established in late 1976, eight of which were subsequently sent to Eritrea.[70]

On the insurgent side in 1976, the power balance between the ELF and the EPLF shifted significantly because, while the later showed better organising abilities, the former fall prey to a new bout of vicious infighting during which numerous fighters were killed, thousands of others mutinied and another 1,200 rallied to the EPLF.[71]

Fall of Nakfa

In mid-1976, the reinforced EPLF launched its first major offensive by attacking a number of isolated Ethiopian garrisons in northern Eritrea. The border town of Karora was besieged and fell on 5 January 1977. Meanwhile, up to 3,000 insurgents were concentrated in the Nakfa area, a small town in the mountainous and sparsely populated Sahel region, which turned into the main rear base of the entire movement. The town was attacked on 17 September 1976 but 297 men of the 15th Infantry Battalion of the Ethiopian Army led by Major Mammo Tarnteme, repulsed the first assault with help of air support provided by F-86Fs of what had, meanwhile, been re-designated as the Ethiopian Air Force (EtAF). One of EtAF's jets was shot down, but its pilots managed to eject.

In an attempt to reinforce the Nakfa garrison, transports of the air force were deployed to drop 100 paratroopers of the Airborne Brigade. With close air support provided by fighter-bombers these troops managed to seize a few hilltops surrounding Nakfa in turn enabling the UH-1Hs of the Army Aviation to deploy an additional 30 troops and evacuate wounded. Despite this success the HQ of the 2nd Division in Asmara then ordered the garrison to reduce its defensive perimeter and withdraw to the outskirts of the agglomeration. In late September, two relief attempts were made by two different Neblebal battalions, but both were repulsed. A third attack was launched by an entire brigade in November, but this was ambushed and forced to retreat. Through all of this time the besieged 15th Battalion was submitted to frequent assaults by day and night, or harassment attacks and bombardment from mortars. It survived only thanks to supplies airdropped by EtAF's C-119s. Some supplies landed in insurgent-held areas, while others ended in the no-man's land, in turn triggering bouts of fighting as the EPLF invariably tried to prevent the Ethiopians from retrieving them.

Over the time, pilots of EtAF fighter-bombers continuously increased the precision of their air strikes and para-drops. The insurgents reacted by digging trenches ever closer to the defence position. Because of this, the Ethiopians were constantly on the verge of starvation: indeed, troops often went for three days without receiving anything to eat. Finally, on 22 March 1977, the EPLF made good use of foggy weather – which prevented the EtAF from providing support – to launch a massive attack. Advancing in two waves, with one group dashing to reach Ethiopian positions while another provided covering fire, the insurgents gained a foothold

Both the ELA and the EPLA grew significantly during the times of general disorder in Ethiopia in 1974-1977. Here one of the first large formations of the ELA is seen during preparations for a major operation in the Asmara area in 1975. (Albert Grandolini Collection)

within the defensive perimeter. In the course of their third assault of the day, they began progressing inside the trench system, frequently fighting hand-to-hand against weakened Ethiopian soldiers. Facing a desperate situation, the survivors of the garrison and paratroopers managed to break through enemy lines: only 75 of them reached Afabet, on 25 March 1977.[72]

Growth of Insurgency

Regardless of the heroic defence of its garrison, the fall of Nakfa had deep psychological impact. It raised the morale of the insurgents and lowered that of the Ethiopian troops in Eritrea. It marked a turning point in the war, and emboldened the EPLF to launch other attacks on towns in order to link-up the areas under its control with those in the densely populated rural areas of the central highlands.[73]

A string of further victories followed: Afabet and Elabered were captured in early April 1977, thus cutting off two of the three roads connecting Keren with Asmara. Three months later, the EPLF was strong enough to launch simultaneous attacks against Keren and Decamere, south of Asmara.

Because that town was heavily protected, the attack on Keren was carefully prepared. Insurgent informers studied the defences for weeks, while the EPLF stockpiled large amounts of ammunition and other supplies in order to enable days of intensive fighting. The assault was opened on 1 July 1977 by EPLF forces under the command of Asmarom Gherezghier. They first seized an Ethiopian position on a dominating hill, from where the insurgents could exercise fire control over the adjacent airstrip – thus making it impossible for the EtAF to resupply and reinforce the garrison by air.

On 5 July, assault parties, supported by mortar fire, attacked and captured positions on ridges surrounding Keren and, a day later, opened their attack into the town itself. Following two days of bitter street-fighting, the surviving Ethiopians retreated into the Italian-built fort on the top of a hill in the centre of Keren, where they refused several calls to surrender. Left without a choice, the insurgents launched their final assault on 8 July, after a severe artillery preparation, and overcame the last defenders. The EPLF subsequently claimed to have killed 2,000 and captured 1,784 Ethiopian troops in exchange for 300 of their own killed. While this was one of rare instances in which the insurgents admitted and reported own losses, it was not the first in which they published wildly exaggerated reports about Ethiopian casualties: after Nakfa, they claimed to have killed 840 Ethiopian soldiers – which was nearly twice the garrison's total strength at its peak.[74]

With a combined ELF-EPLF assault resulting in the capture of Decamara, on 6 July 1977, Addis Ababa's control over Eritrea was seriously threatened – even more so because a few days later Somalia invaded Ogaden. Indeed, the situation deteriorated even further, as the military withdrew some of its units, while the insurgents took Segeneiti and Digsa along the road connecting Decamare with Adi Keyh, in early August 1977, and Umm Hajar, Tessenei, Agordat, Mendefera, and Addi Quala by the mid-August. Furthermore, an Ethiopian Army unit moving along the road to Decamare was ambushed near Adi Hawesha, just a dozen kilometres outside Asmara, and suffered heavy casualties. Overall, by September 1977, Addis Ababa controlled only Asmara, Massawa, Asseb, Barentu and Senafe, and a few crucial positions along the road connecting Asmara with Massawa.[75]

Ethiopia received nine Fairchild C-119K Packet transports, starting in 1971. The type saw intensive service during the war in Eritrea, where it was deployed to haul reinforcements and supplies to Asmara and Massawa, but also as an airborne command post. The last Ethiopian C-119s were replaced by Soviet-made Antonov An-12s in the early 1980s. (Albert Grandolini Collection) Caption:

Organisation of the EPLF

In addition to the general disorganization of the Ethiopian military, and the Somali invasion of Ogaden, another important reason for the success of the Eritrean insurgency in 1977 were reforms of the latter, introduced in the course of the I Congress of the EPLF, held in January of that year. In the course of that meeting, a 37-member Central Committee was elected, which in turn elected 13 individuals to form a Politburo. The latter was composed of the EPLF's Secretary General, Ramadan Muhammad Nur; his deputy, Isaias Afewerki, and eleven other members, each of whom presided over the movement's major committees and departments. The Politburo was not permanently active, and delegated the day by day decision-making to a four member standing committee composed of the secretary general, the vice-secretary general, and the leaders of the Military and Political committees. The EPLF thus turned into an organization that strictly followed the Leninist pattern of democratic centralism.[76]

Furthermore, the EPLF progressively expanded its political-military organisation – in which, as ever since its inception, most of its top cadres occupied alternatively, or even simultaneously, civilian as well as military functions – and took great care to rally the support of civilians and control them. In government-controlled areas, this organization remained clandestine, but it operated overtly in insurgent-controlled zones, and it proved instrumental for overall success of the EPLF because it was providing the organization with intelligence, labour, food, pack animals and recruits. Through providing basic medical services and schools, and with majority of its members remaining uncorrupted, the movement was very successful in gaining public consent. Indeed, through the Eritrean Relief Association (ERA) – established already in 1975 – it proved highly efficient in obtaining help from Western non-governmental organizations (NGOs), and even managed to alleviate starvation in the insurgent-controlled areas.[77]

The EPLF's security structure was highly efficient, tightly controlled and generally secretive. It not only included a secret political party – the Eritrean People's Revolutionary Party (EPRP) led by Isaias Afewerki, staffed by hand-picked insurgents and top commanders, and maintaining its own structures - but also two efficient intelligence and security organizations. Led by Petro Salomon, the Department of Military Intelligence (also known as 'Brigade 72') was responsible for external intelligence and ran networks of informers in government-controlled areas, Eritrean communities abroad, in the Ethiopian armed forces, and in rival insurgent movements. The Department of Internal Security (also 'Halewa Sawra', or 'Defence of the Revolution'), led by Ali Said Abdalla, was responsible for counter-intelligence operations and

Eritrean insurgents before launching an attack on Ethiopian positions, in 1977. (Albert Grandolini Collection)

Isaias Afewerki (left) inside an underground bunker in Nakfa, in 1979. (Photo by Dan Connell)

EPLA's recruits undergoing training in 1978. (Photo by Dan Connell)

Training of female recruits in the 'base-area' of the EPLA in 1979. (Photo by Dan Connell)

enforcing internal discipline. Known as the 'Hidden Ghosts', its members were widely feared in the entire movement.[78]

Another of the strengths of the EPLF was its robust training system, which allowed dramatic expansion of its military wing during the 1970s and 1980s. Each male recruit underwent a six month training course during which – reflecting the dual nature of the EPLF – he was submitted to political education and military training in groups of 60 to 70 trainees supervised by one political and one military instructor. At the end of the course the new recruits were submitted to an exam; if they failed they had to follow the whole session again. The regimen was very intensive and introduced the newcomers to a word of harsh living conditions and very strict discipline. Women – which composed as much as one third of the movement and made up to 15% of combat units – and boys underwent longer training, lasting up to nine months.[79]

Initially, all recruitment was on a volunteer basis, but as the movement expanded and had to replace increasing losses, the communities under insurgent-control were coerced into providing a pre-determined number of recruits, starting in 1981. Eventually, even a universal conscription was introduced.[80]

EPLF's military wing was organised along a classic Maoist layered pattern. With this, local part-time militias were raised: these were lightly-armed and didn't benefit from extensive training. Although normally not mobile, they proved vital assets and had a vast array of missions. Present in insurgent- as well as in government-controlled areas, they could eliminate any governmental civilian structures in their zone, help the EPLF mass organisations to control the local population, harass police and army units, sew mines or sabotage transportation and communication infrastructures, thus tying down army units which would had been very useful somewhere else. Starting in 1981, these militias began to be organised in Zonal Armies (Zobawi Serawit) and with time, the efficiency of some of the units in question matched that of their 'regular' counterparts, eventually allowing the formation of entire divisions which were integrated into the movement's conventional order of battle in 1988.[81]

This, 'typically guerrilla' structure was further combined with 'regular', almost conventional forces that developed progressively. Indeed, the conventional arm of the EPLF – the Eritrean People's Liberation Army (EPLA) – was since its inception heavily influenced by the professionalism inherited from the numerous former officers of the Imperial Ethiopian Army who joined the movement after Selassie was overthrown. This is why, from at least 1977, the EPLA de-facto waged a conventional war in association with a guerrilla war; engaging the Ethiopian army in frontal battles while defending its rear bases in the Sahel region. In turn, this prompted the insurgency to pay ever greater attention to training, use of relatively complex weapons systems (like heavy artillery), careful planning, and develop its offensive and defensive tactics.

Like the entire movement, the EPLA was a highly centralised and structured organisation. Until his death in 1985, it responded to the EPLF's Military Commission chaired by Ibrahim Afa – although it allowed for significant tactical flexibility by local commanders.[82]

The total fighting strength of the EPLF increased gradually from a few hundred fighters in the early 1970s, to about 30,000 in 1982, 50,000 in 1987, and peaked to an estimated 80,000-90,000 troops

A large group of youthful Eritrean recruits undergoing basic training in the Nakfa area in 1979. (Photo by Dan Conell)

in the period 1990-1991. EPLF and EPLA's structures evolved accordingly, becoming ever more complex: while between 1970 and 1972 it never operated in larger units than Mesre ('Squad') of 15 combatants, from 1972 'Ganta' ('Platoon') of 45 to 60 insurgents became frequent. A year later, the first Hayli ('Company') of 140 to 200 became operational, including three platoons and a support element, and in 1975 the EPLA organized a three-company-strong Bottoloni ('Battalion'). The first three-battalion-strong brigade appeared in 1977, but there are conflicting reports about their strength – ranging from 400 to 750 per battalion, up to between 1,300 and 2,000 per brigade. Certain only is that as of 1978, the EPLA totalled nine brigades, as listed in Table 4.

Table 4: Brigades of the EPLA, 1978[83]

4th Brigade
8th Brigade
23rd Brigade
31st Brigade
44th Brigade
51st Brigade
58th Brigade
70th Brigade
76th Mechanized Brigade

The build-up of the EPLA's regular formations intensified during the 1980s. Four infantry divisions – each of three brigades and totalling around 7,500 men – were created in October 1984. Four additional divisions followed, two of these in 1986 and two in 1988.

Finally, because of relatively static frontlines and the generally defensive operational posture of the insurgents, the EPLA established four 'Fronts' (Najfa, Halhal, East and South), that controlled all units active within their area of responsibility. In turn, these Fronts were re-organized into Corps-sized formations in February 1991, during preparations for the all-out offensive to expel the Ethiopians from Eritrea.

While the majority of EPLA units were light infantry, the organization pooled all of its heavy weapons into dedicated units. These were attached to other formations as and when necessary, but always on a temporary basis. Similarly, specialised 'commando' units – the Kebritto ('Matches') – were established for commando operations and deep reconnaissance behind enemy lines, and grouped into the dedicated Commando Division, established in 1987. Separately, the Fedayeen units were specialized in covert

operations of sabotage, abduction, and assassination on enemy territory. Such specialized formations remained independent from any Front- and, later Corps-commands: instead, they assigned their sub-units to other forces as necessary.

Finally, while proving unable to establish a flying service, the EPLA did build up a naval branch equipped with small ships and boats. This was primarily tasked with transportation duties.[84]

An overview of the EPLA's order of battle at the times of its maximal mobilisation, in 1991, is provided in Table 5.

Table 5, EPLA Order of Battle, May 1991[85]

Unit	Commanding Officer	Notes
Corps 161	Teklay Habteselassie	
Division 88	Ahmed Dalil	est. 1988
Division 90	Abdu Mehamed	est. 1988
Corps 271	Haile Samuel	
Division 61	Eyob Fesehaye	est. 1984
Division 85	Umar Hassan	est. 1984
Corps 381	Mesfin Hagos	
Division 52	Dilipos Woldeyohannes	est. 1984
Division 96	Sebhatu Like	est. 1984
Corps 491	Saleh Heruy	
Division 70	Tekle Kifle	est. 1986
Division 16	Abrahale Kifle	est. 1986
Independent Formations		
Division 74	Romadan Awliya	Heavy weapons division, est. 1984
Commando Division	Gerezgiher Andemariam	est. 1987
Naval Wing	Mehamed Humed Karikare	

Despite the limited support provided to the EPLF over time by countries like Libya, Iraq, and Syria, and donations from the Eritreans living abroad, the movement invested immensely into becoming

For all of the 1960s and into the 1970s, Eritrean insurgents depended on mostly primitive methods of moving their supplies – with the help of pack-animals, especially camels. It was only after they captured numerous Ethiopian military vehicles, in period 1974-1977, that the use of these became more widespread. This photograph is showing an EPLF caravan moving supplies over rugged terrain in 1979. (Photo by Dan Connell)

The EPLF constantly paid great attention to propaganda work and establishing good ties to the local population – including women. This photograph shows a captured Ethiopian BRDM-2 armoured scout car, used during a demonstration to propagate the emancipation of women, in 1978. (Photo by Dan Connell)

as self-sufficient as possible. Correspondingly, tremendous energy and resources were invested into developing a dense network of hospitals, schools, poultry farms, workshops, prisoner of war camps, and various other infra-structure – especially so in its rear-bases, in the Sahel area. Well dispersed and camouflaged, these facilities produced uniforms and medicine, refurbished captured vehicles and armament, and even launched limited production of basic spares and ammunition for firearms, as well as landmines. Precisely this support infra-structure was to prove crucial for the success of the EPLF and its armed wing in the long run.[86]

Organization of the TPLF

The Tigray People's Liberation Front (TPLF) was founded on 18 February 1975 by a group of leftist students and intellectuals from Tigray. Mixing classic Marxist-Leninist ideology with regionalist agendas, its founders aimed to end the state of backwardness in which Tigray has fallen despite being one of the historic cradles of the Ethiopian civilisation. They opened their armed struggle with operations by a group of only eleven men armed with outdated rifles, that established a base at Dedebit; a hilly area that traditionally served as a refugee for all kind of outlaws. In May 1975, this first group was reinforced by 21 combatants that had undergone training in Eritrea by the EPLF. However, the support by the Eritreans remained limited: these provided only ten firearms, including two AK assault rifles, eight Simonov rifles and Uzi sub-machine guns, and three hand grenades. Although inexperienced, all the insurgents in question were well-acquainted with the works on people's warfare by such theoreticians as Che Guevara and Mao, and they submitted themselves to rigorous training by Asgede Gebre-Selassie – the only member with soldiering experience (as a former corporal in the IEA).[87]

The TPLF's first armed action took place on 5 August 1975, when 11 fighters attacked the Shire police station to free one of their arrested leaders. Their next move, 'Operation Aksum', was launched on 4 September 1975, when 14 insurgents attacked the Aksum police station and the local bank, and killed four police officers before withdrawing with a booty of 72 rifles and Birr 175,000 in cash.

These two small-scale actions served as a tremendous propaganda coup, and the TPLF quickly became a rallying point for the entire region, easing further recruitment. From then on, the small movement expanded gradually – primarily due to internal tensions that repeatedly erupted between recruits with very different backgrounds.

The movement totalled 126 fighters when it held its I Congress, on 18 February 1976. At the time, its combatants were organized into two platoon-strength companies, or Haili ('Force'): the Haili Woyyane and Haili Dedebit. By July 1976, the TPLF had grown enough to create nine such formations, each with at least 100 combatants organized into three Ganta ('Platoon') with three Mesree ('Squadron'), as listed in Table 6. To prevent disparities in fighting abilities between different units, new recruits were systematically mixed with veterans. Furthermore, the TPLF began creating structures to rally support from the local peasantry.[88]

Table 6: TPLF's Hailis, July 1976

11th Company
21st Company
31st Company
41st Company
51st Company
61st Company
71st Company
81st Company
91st Company

Elimination of Rivals

While the TPLF continued launching small-scale attacks against the government – like the one on Adigrat, on 12 June 1976, when the 11th and 21st Companies destroyed a crack Nebelbal unit – it spent most of this early phase of its existence fighting other insurgent groups present in Tigray. The first rival that was eliminated was the Tigray Liberation Front, which intended to create an independent 'Great Tigray', and was already compromised by deep internal rifts. The group was decapitated when most of its leaders were captured during negotiations with the TPLF, and three of them killed, in November 1975.[89]

Another rival, the Ethiopian Democratic Union (EDU), proved a tougher opponent and took several years to overcome. Founded in 1976 by Ras Mengesha Seyoum, Tigray's last hereditary governor, this was a conservative movement supported by the USA, Saudi Arabia, and Sudan – of which the two former provided financial aid, and the later bases. The TPLF suffered a heavy blow during a fire-fight with combatants of the EDU on 13 June 1976, when Gessesew Ayele – one of its founders and a highly popular figure – was killed. Considering this a 'declaration of war', in mid-July 1976 it deployed the 11th, 21st and 41st Companies to encircle and defeat the rival group and took 134 as prisoners while killing the others. In another mutual clash, on 27 September 1976, both sides suffered heavy casualties, but the TPLF prevailed and forced the Union into a retreat.[90]

Far from being beaten, the conservative movement reorganised itself and recruited thousands of new fighters amongst the sizeable Ethiopian refugee population of southern Sudan. Thanks to external sources of support, these troops were relatively well-equipped with small-arms and mortars too. Probably intending to sweep aside TPLF and to march on Addis Ababa, the EDU launched a major advance into Ethiopia and overwhelmed the garrisons of the border towns like Humera and Metena in early March 1977. Surprised by this resurgence, the TPLF attempted to stop this drive by concentrating

A group of Tigrayan insurgents with captured Ethiopian troops, sometimes in the early 1981. (Albert Grandolini)

seven of its nine companies in the vicinity of Sheraro, where they entrenched themselves. The vastly superior EDU force reached this area on 12 March 1977 and immediately launched a determined attempt to break through. This assault was repulsed, but the battle continued into the next day with the EDU continuing to launch frontal – and very costly – attacks. Eventually, late on 13 March the TPLF exhausted its ammunition and was forced to abandon the position. However, the EDU failed to progress deep into Ethiopia and was left only in possession of the Adiabo and Shire Districts.

Overwhelmed, but undefeated, at Sheraro, the TPLF changed its tactics and launched an insurgency against the EDU, aiming to progressively wear out its rival. Under constant pressure, and due to losses, the discipline in the Union eroded over the next two years, and its fighters became involved in acts of abuse of local farmers. By November 1979, the TPLF felt strong enough to launch a major attack and definitely chase the conservatives out of Tigray.[91]

The last significant rival of the TPLF was the Ethiopian People's Revolutionary Party (EPRP) and its armed wing, the Ethiopian People's Revolutionary Army (EPRA) which, following their defeat in Addis Ababa, attempted to run an insurgency in the countryside. Following a period of building tensions, the EPRA launched an offensive, and expelled the TPLF from the region of Agame in February 1978. However, this proved to be a big blunder, in that by then the latter movement was already battle-hardened. Thus, when two of the TPLF's companies counter-attacked in April, they easily defeated the EPRA. Following another two weeks of infighting, the Revolutionary Party was decisively defeated and forced to withdraw to Eritrea. Although still facing some competition from these and other local groups, the Tigrayan People's Liberation Front was henceforth the primary insurgent group active in that province.[92]

TPLF's Military Organization

In 1979 the TPLF held its I Congress and, following the usual Leninist pattern, established a Politburo as the supreme decision body. This controlled the political, military and socio-economic committees, which in turn were in charge of further departments. Applying a Maoist pattern, the movement then established a number of mass organisations and basic public services (including schools) and aid organisations (like the Relief Society of Tigray), in order to obtain support of the local population.

Following EPLF's example, the TPLF established its own security branch, the Halewa Weyane ('Defence of the Revolution'), and a clandestine party (the Marxist-Leninist League of Tigray), centred around the Front's most committed members. Remaining pragmatic, the Front took great care not to push too far in regards of social and land reforms, in order not to antagonize generally conservative feelings of the population.[93]

TPLF's military wing was put under the control of the Military Commission: this oversaw the Departments 00 (Intelligence), 02 (Training), and 09 (Logistics), and the movement of units that were divided into three categories: the Woyenti ('Rebels') were static village militias, while the KIbrit ('Matches') and Sheeg ('Torches') were mobile units that conducted small-scale operations against government forces, although remaining responsible to police civilian population, recruitment and conduct of propaganda operations.

By 1982, the TPLF grew to around 6,000 regulars, called Haji. These were organized into battalions, then – as the movement grew in size and power – brigades and, finally, divisions, with between 3,000 and 4,000 combatants each, in 1989. By 1990, the TPLF was able to deploy as many as six divisions organized into two Fronts, as listed in Table 7.[94]

Table 7: TPLF's Divisions, July 1989[95]

Alula Division
Aurora Division
Aqazi Division
Maebel Division
Makdela Division
May-Day Division

The TPLF's military strategy was markedly different to that of the EPLA: it put a premium on mobile guerrilla warfare and generally preferred to withdraw when confronted by strong government forces instead of being drawing into positional warfare – even if this sometimes forced it into the evacuation of important bases. While the Front's leadership included no former high-ranking officers, a number of efficient military commanders emerged over the years, foremost amongst them such as Hadush Araya and Samora Yunus, and they proved instrumental for developing tactics that became trademarks of the organization.

Primary of the TPLF's trademarks was the Qoretta ('splitting apart'): tactics consisting of an infiltration attack on enemy positions with five separate groups, supported by a heavy weapons group. The primary target of the infiltrated group was the HQ: once this attack had sewn confusion, two other groups would either launch flanking attacks, or assault specific points in the enemy lines, while the last group served as a reserve. Generally, the TPLF was adept at

Weapons training of youngsters that joined the EPLA in 1979. (Photo by Dan Connell)

infiltrating and/or isolating different enemy formations or positions before delivering the major blow.

While ambushing convoys, the TPLF generally established blocking positions in the front and the rear with the aim of paralyzing the enemy column, before attacking it from two sides. Its fighters sought to close-in as fast as possible and then swarm split and reduce the enemy. Furthermore, the TPLF was adept at deception and psychological warfare, and frequently rotated its units to create the impression of being stronger than in reality, or to entice enemy to disperse its troops.[96]

Contrary to the EPLF, which held its prisoners of war virtually until the end of war, the TPLF 're-educated' and 're-trained' as many of them as possible, usually for four to eight months, before letting them decide to join the insurgency, go to Sudan as refugees, or return home. Over the time, this practice enticed many of government's troops to surrender, knowing they would not be mistreated.[97] Finally, and just like the EPLF, the TPLF went to great extents in order to ensure as much self-sufficiency as possible.

CHAPTER 4
ETHIOPIAN ARMED FORCES OF THE 1970s AND 1980s

The Ogaden War between Ethiopia and Somalia, and the alliance between Addis Ababa and Moscow officially established in November 1977, had drastic effects upon the entire Ethiopian military. Foremost, the Soviet agreement to provide almost unlimited support in regards of arms, enabled the Derg to launch a massive expansion of the armed forces. While ground forces and the navy profited most from this development, this came at significant cost; on the contrary, the Ethiopian Air Force proved much more cautious while making its own experiences from cooperation with the Soviets.

Expansion of the Army
Starting with August 1977, the Ethiopian military was put under the control of the National Revolutionary Operations Command (NROC), re-named into the Military Operations and Planning Command (MOPC), in early 1982. This was a 28-member council chaired by Mengistu Haile Mariam. Generally, the Derg followed a dual policy of activating two categories of ground units: a conventional army, and a quickly-trained militia that filled a constantly increasing requirement for 'boots on the ground'. Further, specialized types of units emerged too, as exemplified by the simultaneous appearance of the elite Nebelbal forces and the local militias, during the Operation Raza, in 1976.[98]

Facing the looming Somali invasion, in early 1977 the Derg mobilized dozens of thousands of farmers, and sent all of these to the newly-established Camp Tataq ('Get Armed'), where they were trained with the help of Cuban instructors. The first of the resulting units – totalling no less than 70,500 combatants organized into 30 brigades – completed their training in late June of the same year. They were followed by the second 'wave', which entered its training in September 1977 and resulted in the creation of 31 brigades. These forces were instrumental for formation of ten infantry divisions between 1977 and 1979, followed by seven established in the period 1989-1991.[99]

Meanwhile, the Army operated the four infantry divisions existent since before 1974, and activated its fifth formation of this size in 1977. Each of these included three or four brigades, each of which was nominally 2,099 strong and including four battalions of 426 each. Supported by four 82mm mortars, three B-10 recoilless guns and three teams equipped with 9M14 (AT-3 Sagger) anti-tank missiles, the Ethiopian Army's infantry battalions became reasonably well-equipped. However, infantry brigades lacked their own artillery. Furthermore, there was significant diversity in the order of battle of different divisions, as brigades and battalions were attached or rotated to reinforce different frontlines or replace exhausted formations.

Except for the five infantry divisions, thanks to the mass influx of Soviet-made arms, the Army was able to establish a number of independent artillery, engineer, anti-aircraft, and tank battalions. Six of the latter were deployed in Eritrea alone by 1983, together with four independent mechanized brigades (the 6th, 16th, 27th and 29th). Each of these had a nominal strength of 2,546 officers and other ranks, and consisted of three mechanized battalions with 22 Soviet-made BTR-60 APCs, an armoured battalion with 22 T-55 MBTs (divided into three companies of 7 tanks each), and an artillery battalion with 12 122mm D-30 howitzers. These four brigades were considered the elite and thus carefully trained and maintained.[100]

New airborne and commando units were activated too, in addition to further Nebelbal formations – all of which were merged into the 6th Division in 1977. Training of the 1st, 2nd and 3rd Para-Commando Brigades began in August 1977, but was not completed by the time these were rushed to the frontlines, late the same year. The 5th Airborne Brigade was activated in March 1983, and was followed by three formations of similar size and purpose – and these were all put under the command of the 102nd Airborne Division in August 1985. The 103rd Commando Division, the formation of which began in January 1987, was followed by establishment of two hastily trained airborne divisions over the next two years. Furthermore, in November 1988, North Korean instructors began training the first three 2,000-strong 'Sparta Brigades', designated 1/81/1, 1/81/2, and 1/81/3. Five other batches of three brigades followed until 1991, bringing the total of these 'Sparta brigades' to 18.[101]

Complete order of battle of the Ethiopian ground forces in the period 1977-1991, is provided in Table 8.

Manning the Colossus
The accelerated growth of Addis Ababa's military apparatus had other consequences which contributed to its demise. In a typical vicious circle, the military expenses increased enormously, from 18% of the total government budget in 1974 to 44% in 1988 with adverse effects upon the economy. Under the Derg, combined budgets for education, health, agriculture and industry were barely half of the amounts invested in the military. Meanwhile, the economic growth of 4% of the GNP between 1977 and 1982 fell to less than

Ethiopian relations with the Soviet Union were strongly influenced by good relations between Mengistu Haile Mariam and the Cuban leader Fidel Castro. The latter pressed hard for Moscow to provide an army for Addis Ababa, and encouraged Soviets even further through deploying his armed forces in Ethiopia. This still from a video shows Mengistu and Castro during one of military parades in Addis Ababa in 1978. (Albert Grandolini Collection)

Recruits of the People's Militia undergoing training in 1977. (Albert Grandolini Collection)

Thanks to advice of Cuban military advisors, Camp Tatek was turning out dozens of thousands of new soldiers for the Ethiopian Army and various para-military forces starting in 1977. Here a column of soldiers are shown, decorated with Cuban and Ethiopian flags, during their graduation ceremony. (Albert Grandolini Collection)

1% during the following years.[102] Unsurprisingly, the government grew less and less popular and further aggravated the situation by committing several blunders that antagonised ever larger parts of the rural populations. A large-scale program of forced resettlement of peasant communities began to be implemented in November 1984, when the government-owned Agricultural Marketing Corporation (established in 1976 and renowned for its endemic corruption) began forcing peasants to sell their products below market rates. Subsequent draught, combined with disorganisation and ongoing war, caused a mass starvation in 1984.[103]

The loss of the government's popularity had far-reaching consequences for the military too. While at earlier times they had enough volunteers to fill its ranks, recruitment became ever harder afterwards. For example, the number of soldiers enlisted in the People's Militia fell from 97,250 in 1979 to only 32,970 in 1989.[104]

The recruitment crisis enticed the government to compensate for the declining input of volunteers for the regular army by introducing conscription in May 1983. Draftees were subjected to a six months training period and then had to serve another two years before being discharged. The conscription system was unfair because of corruption and various exemptions which often allowed men from well-situated families to avoid to be drafted altogether. Unsurprisingly, conscription became unpopular to the point that cases of self-mutilation to avoid military service were reported.[105]

For training of new recruits, the army established four major camps by 1987, baptised Tatek 2, 3, 4 and 5 after the first Camp Tatek. Combined, these had a capacity of training up to 100,000 soldiers a year, but such figures were never reached: 38,949 conscripts completed their training in September 1984, and about 500,000 by 1991. However, these camps had poor sanitation facilities, and recruits were provided with a poor diet, which led to widespread disease, while the quality of training varied from camp to camp. Over time, desertion became endemic: no fewer than 3,184 recruits disappeared already by May 1984.[106]

Another problem that marred the Ethiopian military was the rivalry between the regular army and other paramilitary formations. While the army soldiers were allocated a monthly salary of at least Birr 177, militiamen and conscripts received mere 20 and 19.50 a month, respectively. Furthermore, People's Militiamen – who were initially subjected to the Ministry of Interior, before being transferred under the command of the Ministry of National Defence – often felt that the army officers considered them as mere cannon fodder. In the light of such problems, it is unsurprising that the army fell short by 62,396 troops from its allocated manpower of 313,148 in November 1987 – only a short while before the decisive series of battles in Eritrea. Although its authorised strength was increased to 373,782 regular soldiers by late 1989 (plus 72,199 in the People's Militia), fact was that by the time the Ethiopian Army was suffering unsustainable attrition.[107]

Shattered Officer Corps

During the times of Emperor Selassie's regime, the Ethiopian military emphasised quality over quantity. Expansion of the Ethiopian Army from 1977 onwards thus created incredible problems with regards to recruiting and training officers and various specialists. The outputs of the Holata and Harar Military Academies (which ran one-year-long lieutenant courses) and the Military School of Hurso (which trained non-commissioned officers for six months) were woefully inadequate. By the mid-1980s, the army lacked thousands of officers: indeed, most combat units lacked nearly 50% of their officer-allocations.

The army command reacted by emphasising quantity over quality: training courses for new lieutenants were slashed by half, and then by two thirds. At higher ranks, although a new Staff Academy was established in Addis Ababa in 1985, all officers were sent to the USSR for further training.[108]

Similar difficulties were encountered with regards to technicians, medical personal and other specialists, as the specialised schools, such as the Mulugeta Buli Technical School, were insufficient to train enough personnel. The shortage of medical personnel was such that fully qualified doctors were available only in the three

Amongst the arms impressed upon Ethiopia by the Soviets in the late 1977, were five battalions of S-75 (SA-2 Guideline) …

… and four of S-125 (SA-3 Goa) surface-to-air missile systems. While certainly making an impressive appearance on parades like this one in Addis Ababa of 1978, these expensive weapons that required training of thousands of personnel in the USSR, proved entirely useless. After the Ogaden War – during which its air force destroyed that of Somalia – Ethiopia never faced any kind of a serious aerial threat again. (Albert Grandolini Collection)

main military hospitals, while the entire army had fewer than 400 trained nurses and doctors in 1980.[109]

Still, the worst of the failures that plagued the Ethiopian military was inflicted by the Derg. To protect himself from a possible coup, Mengistu imposed a triangular command structure: in addition to the classic military hierarchy, the entire pyramid was repeated on the political and security plan, and each of these three systems depended on an entirely different chain of command. The Military Security Organisation (MSO), created in 1980, was led by Brigadier-General Abebe G. Meskel, and controlled security officers. The Main Political Administration of the Revolutionary Armed Forces (MPA), was led by Brigadier General Gabreyes Wolde Hana and controlling political commissars. Correspondingly, at various levels of the hierarchy, a military commander, a political officer and a security officer all had the same powers, although the military commander usually being the senior to the other two. As a result, these three had to establish a consensus before any decision could be taken. The triangular system had a highly deleterious effect on the officer corps and wasted the talents of numerous highly trained and experienced high-ranking officers that were one of the army most precious assets.[110]

Captain Tarekegn Almaw described the system as one that,

… undermined discipline, command and control, destroyed self-confidence of commanders, promoted divisiveness, devalued and squandered time, eliminated any sense of responsibility, wasted intelligence, promoted self-interest, and gave priority to political loyalty over military duty and performance.

Mengistu made things even worse with his predilection for micro-management. He often by-passed the command structure to issue direct orders, while keeping his control as strict as possible. Eventually, his approval became mandatory for movement of even a single brigade.[111]

The triangular command system had particularly adverse effects upon the Military Intelligence Department. Instead of monitoring enemy activities, this organisation spent significant resources on spying upon its own military. This flaw was worsened by the lack of properly trained officers, and by the relative neglect the service suffered during the first few years of the Derg rule.

Foreign Advisors

During the 1970s and 1980s the Soviet Army deployed hundreds of military advisors to Ethiopia. About 1,900 of these arrived during the Ogaden War, and were appointed to virtually all of the Ministry of National Defence's main departments, as well as in all of the major army commands.[112]

Relations between Ethiopian and Soviet personnel were often tense, the former frequently resenting the high-handiness and arrogance of the latter. Such feelings were not reserved for lower ranks. Even the relations between Lieutenant-General Tasfaye Gabra-Kidan (Ethiopian Minister of Defence from 1980 until 1985 and a well-respected strategist popular in the Army) and top Soviet advisors were strained by near-constant disagreements over strategy and tactics – especially planning advocated by the latter.[113]

Eventually, Ethiopians concluded that they often benefited more from the presence of advisors and contingents from allies other than from the Soviets. East Germany provided advice in regards of different security services, helped organise logistical support for many of the operations in Eritrea and Tigray of the late 1970s, and trained Mengistu's personal guard – the four-battalion-strong Special Defence Brigade.[114]

Much more important became the Cuban presence. No less than 3,000 Cuban troops arrived in Ethiopia in November and December 1977. They proved instrumental for training the People's Militia and helping the Army adapt recently delivered Soviet heavy weaponry. The Cuban contingent – which peaked at around 15,000

Most heavy armament sold by Moscow to Ethiopia was literally '2nd hand': weapons systems that were considered surplus to requirements of the Soviet Army. One exception to this rule were ZSU-23-4 Shilka self-propelled, radar-supported, quadruple anti-aircraft cannons. During the war in Ethiopia, they proved highly effective against enemy infantry. (Albert Grandolini Collection)

troops during the following months – also took direct part in the Ogaden War.

However, following Somalia's defeat, Cuban leader Fidel Castro refused to have his troops engaged against what was considered 'internal opponents'. Because Eritrea was considered a part of Ethiopia, Cubans thus never saw any combat in that part of the country.

The Cuban contingent had been reduced to between 11,000 and 13,000 by 1981: of these around 8,000 were combat troops who staffed four brigades that served as a deterrent against Somalia, while others served as instructors. Two of the brigades in question were armoured formations: one of them garrisoned Dire Dawa, and the other Jijjiga. A mechanised infantry brigade was based at Camp Tatek, near Addis Ababa, where the HQ of the Cuban contingent was deployed too. Finally, the fourth Cuban brigade – an artillery unit – was deployed in the Jijjiga area too. Each of the formations in question was more powerful than any Ethiopian brigade: armoured formations had three tank battalions with 32 T-54 or T-55 MBTs each, and one mechanized battalion with 31 or 32 BMP-1s. Furthermore, each of these brigades had one artillery battalion with 18 D-30 howitzers, one MRL-battalion with 12 BM-21 launchers, and two anti-aircraft batteries with a total of eight ZSU-23-4 self-propelled anti-aircraft guns. The mechanised infantry brigade consisted of three mechanized infantry battalions, each of which had three companies with 10 BTR-60PB APCs and one artillery battery with six D-30s. The same brigade also had one MRL-battalion and one tank battalion attached. Finally, the artillery brigade had two field artillery battalions with 12 130mm M-46 guns, one howitzer battalion with 12 D-30s, and one MRL battalion with the usual 12 BM-21s. Altogether, and in the regional context, the Cuban contingent, although numerically small, was a powerful and well-equipped force.[115]

While all the heavy equipment operated and maintained by these units was owned by the Ethiopian government, the Cubans had their own logistical system entirely separated from the Ethiopian military. Nevertheless, the Cubans maintained a far better relationship with the Ethiopians than the Soviets ever did, and their relationship with the local population was generally good too. On the negative side, Cuban soldiers – who generally served two-year-long tours of duty in Ethiopia – suffered from low morale and some were engaged in trafficking, including Khat, to earn hard currency.[116]

Moscow's Mixed Blessings

As a result of its alliance with Moscow, Ethiopia received immense amounts of various military supplies from the USSR and other Communist countries. Between 1974 and 1981, military equipment worth about US$ 9.420 billion were delivered: nearly 90% of this was provided on credit, as only equipment worth about US$ 360 million was paid in cash. Furthermore, the Soviets and allies donated material valued at another US$ 727 million. Altogether, during this period, Ethiopia received 1,767 MBTs, 1,665 APCs and infantry fighting vehicles (IFVs), 1,188 artillery pieces, 400 multiple rocket launchers (MRLs), dozens of thousands of different vehicles, 3,621 mortars, 2,321 anti-aircraft guns, dozens of thousands of machine guns, and more than 1.5 million of rifles. Most of the arms acquired in this fashion were of designs from the 1940s, 1950s, and 1960s; for example, Soviet-made T-34/85, T-54, T-55, T-62 MBTs, and North-Korean-made Chonma-ho tanks, BTR-152 and BTR-60 APCs, and BRDM-1 and BRDM-2 armoured reconnaissance vehicles.

The first part of the Ethiopian military to feel the impact of all these deliveries was the Main Logistics Department. This controlled six main branches – including the engineering, logistics, foreign aid, acquisitions, military storage and transport. While generally able to provide reasonably effective support even for ever larger operations undertaken on different battlefields, this service was plagued by important deficiencies that grew ever worse with the time. Except for experiencing constant problems with acquisition and deliveries of spares, the department had to grow at a very fast pace while, just like the rest of the military, it could not train enough specialised personnel.

The Main Logistic Department suffered a constant lack of vehicles. To alleviate this, it began hiring civilian vehicles and drivers, who were frequently unwilling to put their trucks – which they often owned – at risk. Lack of roads in much of Ethiopia further complicated the problem. As a result, Ethiopian troops in Eritrea were often short on food: on one occasion in November 1986 the entire contingent there had only stocks for 24 hours. This situation put an increased strain upon the air force, which had to fly an ever increasing number of resupply flights with its transports and helicopters.

Clearly the small number of qualified military engineers and technicians inherited from the Emperor's times could hardly cope with such an influx, despite their excellent training. In a country with a limited pool of civilians with the necessary skills to draw on, it took years to train enough new engineers and mechanics to properly care about the vast array of weapons and vehicles of Soviet design. Nevertheless, the Soviets continued delivering while proving anything other than helpful with solutions for all the problems the Ethiopians were facing. On the contrary: Moscow took great care to keep Ethiopia dependent on its advice and provision of arms and thus refused to help develop local maintenance facilities, or even to provide technical documentation in the English language. It also proved very difficult to obtain spare parts from the USSR: the Soviets would usually provide a limited amount on delivery, and then refused to deliver any more, and dictated the replacement of entire sub-assemblies instead. In most of cases, this meant that heavy equipment had to be shipped back to the USSR for overhauls – which was a costly and time-consuming process. Ethiopian military experts calculated that the USD$ 142 charged by the Soviets for refurbishing one engine of an APC in the USSR, could have been reduced to USD$ 52, if the same work would had been done in Ethiopia. While most arms were obtained on credit, spare parts – assemblies and sub-assemblies – had to paid for in cash, if Moscow did not refuse to deliver them. For example, out of 6,423 items requested by the Ethiopians between 1985 and 1987, the Soviets delivered only 3,559. Even if an order for spares was accepted, nobody was ready to tell the Ethiopians when these would be delivered. Unsurprisingly, the Ethiopian military lost scores of heavy vehicles because of maintenance-related issues, and general availability of its vehicle park was constantly low.[117]

Addis Ababa took steps to reduce this uncomfortable dependence, and eventually turned to North Korea for help in establishment of an indigenous armament industry. However, of the three projects that were in development, only the work on the Gafat Engineering Plant and the Hormat Project were launched, shortly before the fall of the Derg in 1991. The first was to produce small arms and the second mortar and artillery shells of various calibres, but both came too late to help to compensate for the gradual diminution of the support provided by an increasingly economically ruined Soviet Union.[118]

Table 8, Ethiopian Army and other Ground Forces, 1977-1991

Unit	Date of Establishment	Notes
1st Infantry Division	1950s	former IEA
2nd Infantry Division	1950s	former IEA
3rd Infantry Division	1960s	former IEA, nicknamed 'Lion Division'; including 9th, 10th, 11th and 12th Brigades
4th Infantry Division	1960s	former IEA
5th Infantry Division	1977	People's Militia units
6th Division	1977	Neblebal units
7th Infantry Division	1977	People's Militia units
8th Infantry Division	1977	68th, 91st and 94th Brigades; People's Militia units
9th Infantry Division	1977	People's Militia units
10th Infantry Division	1977	People's Militia units
11th Infantry Division	1977	People's Militia units
12th Infantry Division	1977	People's Militia units
13th Infantry Division	1977	People's Militia units
14th Infantry Division	1978-1979	People's Militia units
15th Infantry Division	1978-1979	People's Militia units; nicknamed 'Nabro'
16th Infantry Division	1978-1979	People's Militia units
17th Infantry Division	1978-1979	People's Militia units; nicknamed 'Tarb' ('Wasp')
18th Mountain Infantry Division	1980	35th, 36th, 37th, and 38th Mountain Infantry Brigades
19th Mountain Infantry Division	1980	39th, 40th, 41st Mountain Infantry Brigades
20th Infantry Division	1980-1981	
21st Mountain Infantry Division	1981	44th, 45th, 46th, 47th Mountain Infantry Brigades
22nd Mountain Infantry Division	1981	48th, 49th, 50th, 51st Mountain Infantry Brigades
23rd Infantry Division	1981-1982	
24th Infantry Division	1981-1982	
102nd Airborne Division	1985	5th, 6th, 7th and 8th Airborne Brigades
1st Mechanized Division	1985-1987	
2nd Mechanized Division	1985-1987	
103rd Commando Division	1987	training began in January 1987
3rd Mechanized Division	1988	
4th Mechanized Division	1988	
204th Airborne Division	1989-1990	
205th Airborne Division	1989-1990	
5th Mechanized Division	1989-1991	
25th Infantry Division	1989-1991	
26th Infantry Division	1989-1991	
27th Infantry Division	1989-1991	
28th Infantry Division	1989-1991	
29th Infantry Division	1989-1991	
30th Infantry Division	1990-1991	formed from released POWs
31st Infantry Division	1990-1991	Formed from released POWs

Most Ethiopian T-28Ds wore a livery consisting of silver grey on engine cowling, top surfaces of the fuselage and all of the fin, and top and bottom surfaces of the wing, and matt white on the sides of the fuselage. At least two were left in bare metal overall. Perhaps as result of combat damage, this example was last sighted with a mix of both: engine cowling, both wing surfaces and the tip of the fin in silver grey, top surfaces of the fuselage in bare metal, and fuselage sides in matt white. National markings were worn in six positions, while its original serial (i.e. the USAF-style FY-number) was rudely oversprayed in light grey (FS36622) and the IEAF/EtAF serial applied above it instead. The aircraft is illustrated in weapons configuration most frequently deployed during the war in Eritrea of late 1960s and early 1970s, including a pair of Mk.82 bombs and a gunpod containing the Browning M2 machine gun and its calibre 7.92mm ammunition. (Artwork by Tom Cooper)

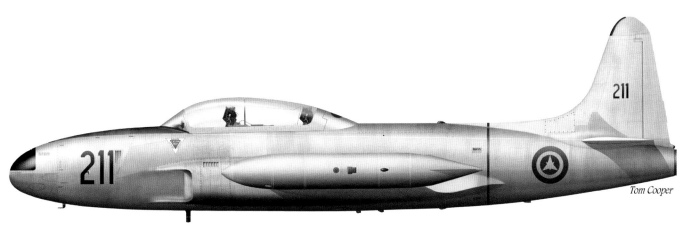

Ethiopia received a total of 14 T-33As from the USA, and 2 RT-33As from The Netherlands. All were assigned to the 33rd Training Squadron and wore the usual 'bare metall overall' livery. As far as is known, national insignia was applied in six position: most have had their serials applied in style as shown here: big, three-digit number in black on the forward fuselage, repeated on the fin. The 33rd Training Squadron served as an operational conversion unit and was deployed to Asmara AB during the Ogaden War. However, it remains unknown if the type actually saw any kind of combat in Ethiopia: all the available photographs and videos show that even internal machine guns were removed, and no underwing hardpoints installed. All T-33As and RT-33As were withdrawn from service by late 1978, and their crews re-trained on MiGs.

While majority of F-86Fs delivered to Ethiopia directly from the USA continued serving in their 'bare metal overall' livery until withdrawn from service, ex-Iranian examples were camouflaged in same colours used on ex-Iranian F-5As. These consisted of tan (FS 20400), brown (similar to BS381C/350) and forest green (FS34079) on top surfaces, and light grey (FS36622) on undersurfaces. As far as is known, national insignia was applied in six positions each side of the rear fuselage and top and bottom surfaces of each wing), while serials (always applied in black, with help of stencils) were worn on the bottom of the front fuselage and near the tip of the fin. All external armament was usually attached to inboard underwing pylons. (Artwork by Tom Cooper)

This F-5A donated to Ethiopia by Iran in 1973-1974 period was camouflaged before delivery in tan (FS20400), brown (similar to BS381C/350) and forest green (FS34079) on top surfaces, and light grey (FS36622) on undersurfaces – already before it entered service with the IEAF. Seemingly around the same time, the Ethiopian air force introduced the practice of applying its national markings only in four positions: on each side of the rear fuselage, top surface of the left wing, and undersurface of the right wing. As usually, three-digit serials were applied on the forward fuselage and the fin. This aircraft is illustrated together with weapons most often deployed during the fighting in Eritrea of the 1970s: including a BLU-27 napalm tank on its outboard underwing pylon, a LAU-61 (or M260) pod for 2.75 inch (68mm) unguided rockets (lower left corner), and a (US-made) M117 general-purpose bomb. This aircraft was sold back to Iran in 1985. (Artwork by Tom Cooper)

All eight Ethiopian F-5Es were camouflaged in tan (FS20400), dark brown (FS30140) and forest green (FS34079) applied along the 'Flogger' pattern on top surfaces, and light grey (FS36622) before delivery. This livery was retained for the rest of their service life with the EtAF. Starting in 1978 – and at the time Western air warfare analysts were discussing the possibility of Soviets making use of Western-made weaponry on their aircraft in the case of the World War III, and then capturing one of NATO's air bases in Western Germany – at least one of Ethiopian F-5Es was equipped with underwing hardpoints from MiG-21. This made it compatible with a wide range of Soviet-made weapons, including UB-16-57 rocket pod, illustrated here. Notable is that the old – 'Imperial' – national markings were retained on the four survivors of Ogaden War until at least late 1978. (Artwork by Tom Cooper)

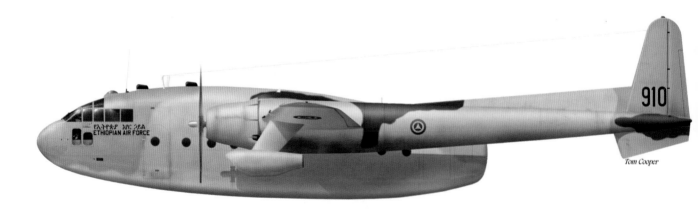

Ethiopia received nine Fairchild C-119K Packer transports and these saw extensive service during the war in Eritrea, remaining in service even once the USSR agreed to sell Antonov An-12s to Addis Ababa, in early 1980s. All were painted in this unique camouflage pattern, apparently consisting of tan, grey and dark green on top surfaces and sides, and light grey on undersufaces. Known serials – always applied in black – were in range from 910 up to 919: the first seven aircraft were eventually abandoned at Debre Zeit, while the last two were sold abroad. Service title was always applied (in Amharic and in English) on either side of the forward fuselage. Except in their basic role, as transporters, C-119s saw extensive service as airborne command posts (Artwork by Tom Cooper)

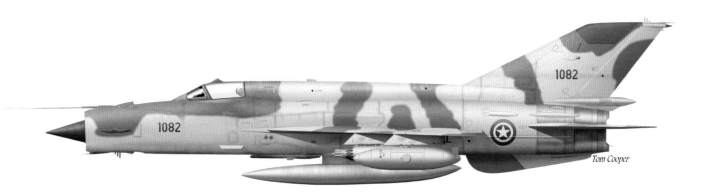

Ethiopia attempted to place its first order for MiG-21bis' already in early 1977. Correspondingly, a group of pilots was sent for conversion training in the USSR in July of the same year. However, negotiations with Moscow lasted several months and were finalized only in November 1977. Deliveries of the first batch of 48 aircraft began only a month later. Further orders issued over the next few years brought the known total to no less than 80. All of these were camouflaged in the standardised pattern applied before delivery, and consisting of beige (BS381C/388) and olive green on upper surfaces and sides, and light admiralty grey (BS381C/697) on undersurfaces. (Artwork by Tom Cooper)

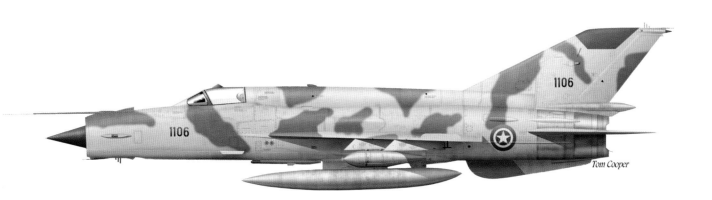

MiG-21bis' delivered to Ethiopia in the early 1980s were still camouflaged in same colours like those delivered in 1977, but beige and olive green were applied in a wide range of diverse patterns. Of interest is that the Ethiopians acquired a wide range of reasonably advanced weapons for their MiG-21bis'. These included not only ZAB-300 and ZAB-500 napalm bombs (illustrated under the outboard underwing pylon of the MiG-21bis '1082' shown above) which the Soviets refused to deliver to any of their customers in the Middle East. The most widely deployed free-fall weapons of the Ethiopian air force were FAB-250M-62 general purpose bombs, one of which is illustrated on the inboard. These calibre 250kg weapons were deployed in thousands. Especially for attacks on EPLF's fortifications, Ethiopian MiG-21bis' often deployed calibre 240mm S-24 unguided rockets. (Artwork by Tom Cooper)

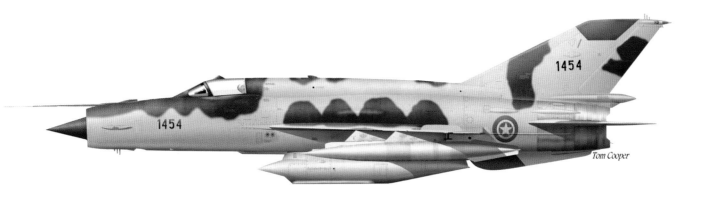

Starting with December 1977, Ethiopia received more than a dozen of MiG-21Rs. These wore serials ranging from 1451 to at least 1464. While some were camouflaged in beige and light earth, others received a pattern consisting of beige and dark green (BS381C/641) instead. Undersurfaces were always painted in light admiralty grey (BS381C/697). As far as is known, MiG-21Rs were usually equipped with D-type pods, containing reconnaissance cameras. Nevertheless, they flew attack sorties too. Carriage of two 400-litre drop tanks on outboard underwing pylons was a 'must' because of long ranges over which they had to operate. Like MiG-21bis', MiG-21Rs should have received national markings in four positions only, but clear photographic evidence remains elusive. (Artwork by Tom Cooper)

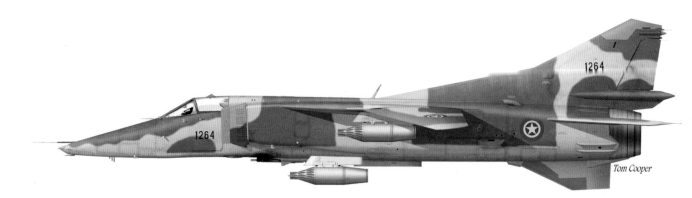

Starting in early 1978, the backbone of the EtAF's fighter-bomber fleet consisted of MiG-23BNs. All the aircraft of the first batch of 44, as well as those delivered during the late 1980s, were camouflaged in beige (BS381C/388), dark brown (BS381C/411 or 450, similar to FS20095), and olive green (BS381C/298, similar to FS34098) on top surfaces and sides, and light admiralty grey (BS381C/697, FS35622) on undersurfaces. Dieletric panels on the nose, top of the fin and along the leading edge of the ventral fin were usually painted in medium grey (FS26152). This dedicated attack variant proved a handful to fly, but was also capable of carrying significant payloads. One of frequently used configurations consisted of four UB-32-57 pods for calibre 57mm unguided rockets. (Artwork by Tom Cooper)

Serials of Ethiopian MiG-23BNs were always applied in black, with help of stencils, on the forward fuselage and the centre of the fin, in range 1251-1303. Like MiG-21bis' before them, they arrived together with large shipments of relatively advanced Soviet-made weapons. Except for RBK-250 cluster bomb units – of which the MiG-23BN could carry up to six at once (as illustrated here) – they were also sighted while carrying slightly larger RBK-250PTABs, but also much heftier RBK-500s. Other frequently used armament included FAB-250M-62 and FAB-500M-62 general purpose bombs, and calibre 240mm R-24B heavy unguided rockets. The latter weapon was preferably deployed against fortified objects – like bunkers. (Artwork by Tom Cooper)

Ethiopia originally acquired 16 MiG-23ML interceptors with intention of bolstering its capabilities against the Somali air force, when this was slowly rebuilt after the Ogaden War. However, the type – operated by Dire Dawa-based 10th Squadron only – was more frequently deployed as fighter-bomber against Eritrean insurgents. All Ethiopian MiG-23MLs were camouflaged in same pattern as that used on MiG-23BNs, and in colours including beige (BS381C/388), dark brown (BS381C/411 or 450, similar to FS20095), and olive green (BS381C/298, similar to FS34098) on top surfaces and sides, and light admiralty grey (BS381C/697, FS35622) on undersurfaces. Dielectric panels like the radome, top of the fin and the leading edge of the ventral fin were painted in medium grey (FS26152). They wore serials in range 1801-1817. (Artwork by Tom Cooper)

Ethiopia acquired two batches of SIAI-Marchetti SF.260TPs: the first one, ordered in 1984, included 11 aircraft; the second, ordered in 1988, included 12 aircraft. All were pained in aluminium overall, and have had their top engine cowlings painted in dark green, and their wing-tip fuel tanks in orange. As far as is known, they were used as basic trainers only – for future Ethiopian Air Force pilots, but also for training of future pilots of the Ethiopian Airlines. (Artwork by Tom Cooper)

A total of 26 Aero L-39C Albatross jet trainers were acquired by Ethiopia, including 10 ordered in 1983, 10 ordered in 1988, and 6 in 1991. They served as basic jet trainers, but also for advanced and even weapons training. Correspondingly, while lacking the internal gun of such dedicated variants like L-39ZA, they did have underwing hardpoints. All Ethiopian L-39Cs were painted in colours known as 5014 (light pastel green) and 5080 (pea green) in the former Czechoslovakia. The latter colour tended to get darker over the time. They seem to have worn the national insignia applied only in two positions, while serials (1701 to 1726) were applied in usual four positions. (Artwork by Tom Cooper)

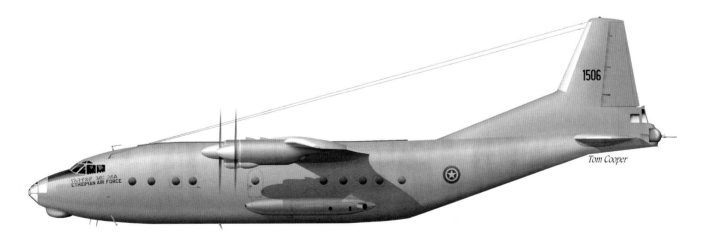

Aiming to replace worn-out C-119s, Ethiopia received 16 Antonov An-12Bs starting in early 1980. All were painted in blue-grey overall, and wore the national insignia in six positions. Big black serials were usually applied on the fin, and full service titles on either side of the cockpit. The latter was usually applied in Amharic and in English, but some examples seem to have received only the English variant. At least two are known to have been written off or shot down over Eritrea: 1509 was shot down in 1982, another example made an emergency landing during the same year, while the empty hulk of 1506 was captured by insurgents at Tesseney, in 1984: apparently, the aircraft was grounded at the local airstrip for unknown reasons, and had all of its useful spares – including engines, propellers, most of windows, and the rear barbette – removed. (Artwork by Tom Cooper)

18 UH-1Hs originally delivered to the Ethiopian Army Aviation were all second-hand Hueys from surplus US Army stocks. They were painted in dark green (FS34086) overall and originally received national markings and yellow titles 'ARMY' on each side of the boom. Reportedly, the first 16 were coded 'EA71-EA87'. However, photographic evidence is available only for their looks after 1977, when new national insignia was applied instead, title 'ARMY' removed, and EtAF-style serial numbers 771-789 applied – in yellow – on the fin. As far as is known they were rarely if ever armed. (Artwork by Tom Cooper)

Gauging by known serials, Ethiopia acquired up to 27 Mi-24s, starting in early 1978 (known serials are in range from 1601 up to 1627). These were pained in in the camouflage pattern known as 'sand and spinach' in the West, which consisted of beige and olive green. Due to intensive service and exposition to the elements, the olive green tended to 'bleach' into various shades of earth colour. Notable is that all the maintenance stencilling on them was in English. This example was last seen at Debre Zeit in the early 1990s, by when it received a replacement upper door for the cabin entry, which never received a coat of camouflage colours. Ethiopian Mi-24s were armed with quite standard arsenal for this type, including UB-32-57 pods for calibre 57mm unguided rockets, but also AT-2 Swatter ATGMs. (Artwork by Tom Cooper)

Ethiopia received a batch of about 20 Mi-8Ts starting in November 1977. All were equipped with sand filters, and painted in sand and light earth on top surfaces and sides, along the pattern shown here. Notable is the big area behind engine exhausts, painted in matt black. Undersides were always painted in light grey, and there are no indications that any national insignia was applied there: instead, this was usually applied on either side of the rear cabin. Serials were always applied in yellow, on the boom: known ones were in range 850 to 865. (Artwork by Tom Cooper)

CKD AH-IV tankettes were developed during the 1930s, along a concept of lightly armoured vehicle carrying a pair of calibre 7.92mm, Skoda ZB heavy machine guns. Ethiopia received a batch starting in 1948: contrary to earlier variants, they had a welded hull and a new, Tatra 114 diesel engine with an increased range and top speed. Due to their reliability, these tankettes saw intensive action in all of conflicts involving Ethiopia and remained in service into the 1980s. From the few photographs that became available over the time, it appears all were painted in olive green overall, and wore small registration plates in yellow on the front and rear hull, as well as turret insignia with unknown background. (Artwork by David Bocquelet)

Ethiopian Army received a batch of 22 M60s in 1974, followed by 11 additional vehicles delivered in 1975. A third batch should have been delivered in 1976 or 1977, bringing the total to 47. All belonged to the original variant, with a turret similar – but not the same – to that of the M48. Next to nothing is known about their subsequent service, except that they seem to have served with the armoured brigade assigned to the 3rd 'Lion' Division, deployed in Ogaden, as of 1977, and that one might have been captured by the Somalis during the Ogaden War. The example in question seems to have been left in Olive Drab overall, and is not known to have worn any kind of markings. (Artwork by David Bocquelet)

A total of 54 M41 Walker Bulldog light tanks were delivered to Ethiopia in late 1960s, and formed an armoured battalion of the original 3rd 'Lion' Division, on its establishment. They saw intensive service during Ogaden War, when several were knocked out in running battles with Somali armour. Most of the 3rd Division is known to have been re-deployed to Eritrea in 1978-1979, but it remains unknown if Ethiopian M41s saw any combat service in that conflict. As far as can be assessed from very few, and usually poor photographs, Walker Bulldogs in service with the Ethiopian Army were all left in olive drab overall, as painted prior to delivery. No turret markings are known to have been applied, except for 5-digit registrations, in white, on turret sides, and the front and the rear of the hull. (Artwork by David Bocquelet)

The first modern APC to enter service in Ethiopia was M75. However, 39 vehicles of this type delivered by the USA in late 1960s proved too heavy, tall, and too expensive, and seem to have been used for training purposes only. A total of 110 M113s were acquired from surplus stocks of the US Army, and assigned to the 3rd 'Lion' Division, starting in 1974. All were left in olive drab livery, as on delivery, but received sizeable insignia on their hull-sides, denoting their assignment to specific mechanised-infantry or self-propelled mortar units. As far as is known, most were out of service by 1980. (Artwork by David Bocquelet)

Ethiopia originally acquired enough T-55s to equip six tank battalions with the type: each of units had a nominal strength of 22 vehicles (distributed into three companies of 7 tanks each). Four of battalions saw action in Eritrea by 1983. Further to this, four mechanised brigades received a battalion of 22 T-55s. Majority of vehicles received no markings or turret insignia at all, and were left in olive green overall. It was only once the EPLF began using some of captured T-55s, that measures for quick identification became necessary – such like addition of a yellow band or the national tricolore around the gun tube, as shown here. (Artwork by David Bocquelet)

Around 200 second-hand, refurbished BTR-60P/PA/PB APCs and about a dozen of BTR-60PBK command vehicles were delivered to Ethiopia from the USSR in 1977 and 1978. Initially, only two armoured brigades entirely staffed by the Cubans were equipped with them. However, by 1982, also four mechanised brigades were equipped with a battalion of 22 vehicles of this type, each. The units in question served as 'armoured fists' in each of major offensives and as fire-brigades whenever the Ethiopians came under pressure. Unsurprisingly, their attrition was heavy: less than 100 remained in service by 1987. As so often, very little is known about the looks of vehicles in question, except that all were painted in olive green overall. (Artwork by David Bocquelet)

Overall, there is no doubt that while the Soviet aid was instrumental in saving the position of the Derg and keeping the Ethiopian military in working condition, in turn it contributed significantly to its final demise too: Moscow not only provided a military apparatus unsustainable by the local economy, and nearly useless for the kind of war in which it was involved, but also kept it dependent on their support – which the Soviets then ceased to provide.

Proud Air Force

The only Ethiopian military service that survived not only the toppling of Emperor Selassie, but all the subsequent power struggles, and then the Ogaden War in largely intact condition – and even experienced a significant and effective growth during the 1970s – was the EtAF. Indeed, following the Ogaden War, even the Derg was particularly proud of the air force and its personnel. Nevertheless, Addis Ababa kept a close eye upon the service and appointed a three-man committee – including its commander, Major-General Fanta Belay, a political commissar, and a representative from the security service – in its command. In 1978, the EtAF was re-organized along the Soviet-style regimental structure, and slightly adapted its national marking through the application of a five-pointed yellow star.

The EtAF ended the war in Ogaden by losing four out of the eight F-5Es it had received from the USA, and nearly all of the remaining T-28s and B.17s. It suffered relatively light losses in personnel, including two F-5-pilots. However, it emerged out of that conflict not only victorious and combat-hardened, but also reinforced by large deliveries of Soviet-made aircraft. This proved a far more problematic issue than one might expect.

As of 1977, the EtAF was no new creation, but an air force with 30 years of uninterrupted history behind it; a closely tied community with its own culture, traditions, doctrine and tactics – and plenty of experience in operating technically complex (and superior) aircraft to those that the Soviets now delivered. Not only were EtAF personnel all literally hand-picked before joining the air force, but nearly all of its officers and other ranks underwent extensive courses and were generally considered – even by their US advisors – as trained to exceptionally high standards. In comparison, their Soviet 'advisors' not only lacked any kind of combat experience, but also proved inferior in their overall levels of tactical and technical knowledge. Unsurprisingly, for most of their times in Ethiopia, Soviet advisors found themselves with very little to do. Somewhat sarcastically, retired EtAF F-5-pilot Berhanu Wubneh later recalled:

Major General Fanta Belay (centre) meeting a group of Army commanders in the late 1970s. Belay commanded the EtAF through most of the 1980s, and was one of the crucial decision-makers in most military-related decisions in Addis Ababa of the times. (EtAF via S. N.)

When the Soviets did arrive, they were most of the times busy copying and carrying away large volumes of all sorts of official EtAF documentation, particularly print-outs related to training and equipment of our aircraft.[119]

Training in the USSR

Moscow permitted Addis Ababa to place its first order for MiG-21bis' supersonic interceptors in spring 1977. Correspondingly, conversion training of Ethiopian pilots to this type was initiated in March of that year, when a team of 20 pilots, 39 specialists and 86 technicians led by Colonel Heilemikael Birru, Major Teshomre Lagesse, and Lietenant Tadesse Raje, respectively, was assembled at Debre Zeit. Split into two groups, the pilots travelled to Moscow via Athens.[120] Following a short stay in Moscow, the entire team was flown to the town of Kusovskye, half an hour drive from Rostov na Donu. Then the pilots were given forms on which they had to list all aircraft they flew, with all of their flight hours. When the forms were turned in, the Russian officers expressed their bewilderment – for reasons that became obvious only later on.

At the Kusovskye air base, the Ethiopians found a number of MiG-21 trainees from Cuba, Tanzania, Uganda and several countries of Eastern Europe. They were given cadet uniforms and advised that the Soviet Union does not recognize ranks of other militaries above sergeant, and that they were to respect every Soviet officer. Unsurprisingly, the Ethiopians refused and insisted upon not standing to attention and saluting anybody below their service rank. A heated argument developed to which no agreement was reached. The Soviets simply decided to class and treat all of Ethiopians – including Colonel Birru – as mere cadets.

The ground training phase was undertaken in well-equipped facilities, with help of interpreters. Immediately after completing their exams, Hailemikael Birru, Berhanu Wubneh, Tesfu Desta, and Neguissie Zergaw were ordered to return to Ethiopia because the situation in Ogaden had heated up. The rest of the team continued with flight training. During this phase, every Ethiopian student pilot was assigned two IPs: all of these were very young and – in comparison to Ethiopians – inexperienced. For example, the instructor assigned to Lieutenant Colonel Gizaw was a captain with a total of 800 hours, whereas Gizaw had over 2,000 hours – of which 1,000 on the F-86 alone. Nevertheless, the Soviet instructor never let him fly on his own – and that from take-off to touch-down. This changed only after Ethiopians complained, and then as they were to fly their first solo flights.

As soon as they soloed, the Ethiopians – used to the USAF's training system – started flying their machines ever more aggressively. Considering such behaviour as 'dangerous', the Soviets gathered the entire team in a classroom. The Soviet regiment commander then explained to everybody:

'There is no fighter aircraft in the world like the MiG-21. It has a record 9:1 win-loss rate against any aircraft. It takes a minimum of nine years to master. Thus, your attempt to go above and beyond what we are teaching you is foolish!'

Overall, in nine months of their conversion course in the USSR, Ethiopian pilots received exactly 25 hours flying time each. Most of this was related to take-offs and landings, with only a few hours devoted to simple manoeuvres and air-to-ground gunnery. To add salt to the injury, as the end of the course neared, the Somalis were in control of almost entire Ogaden and the Soviets began taunting them about a country with 3 million of people achieving such victories against Ethiopia's population of 30 million. Then, just as the two teams completed their training, they received an unexpected

One of the first groups of Ethiopian MiG-21-pilots, as seen in the early 1980s, together with the MiG-21bis' serial number 1055. (EtAF via S. N.)

A brand-new MiG-21bis' as seen shortly after delivery. This aircraft belonged to a batch painted in beige and dark green (see Colour Section for details) on top surfaces and sides. Notable is the application of the serial in fashion characteristic for the Ethiopian Air Force. (EtAF via S. N.)

An Ethiopian pilot with the MiG-21bis' 1059, prior to take-off for a combat sortie. Notable are cordite traces on the lower fuselage, in front of the installation for GSh-23 cannon, indicating heavy use of the latter. (Pit Weinert Collection)

A rare photograph of one of only six Mi-24s originally delivered to Ethiopia in November 1977. Notable is the armament, consisting of UB-32-57 rocket pods, and the serial number 1616 – as well as warning inscription 'Danger' applied on the rear end of the boom, in English. (EtAF via S. N.)

order: some of the pilots were to stay in the Soviet Union for five months longer and convert to MiG-23s. Before their return to Ethiopia, the Soviets forced everybody to turn in their notebooks.

Because nearly all of them were trained in the USA, this relatively short stay in the USSR was an important experience for the Ethiopians. Foremost it showed them that the Soviets were a good way behind in almost every aspect.

Once back in Ethiopia, newly-qualified Ethiopian MiG-21 pilots were still held back by their Soviet advisors. Because of this, and although the type saw intensive combat service during the final phase of the Ogaden War, the overall process of converting the 1st and 2nd Squadrons EtAF to the new type was officially completed only after the end of that conflict. Indeed, both units were officially declared operational only in 1978.

Meanwhile, and as described in detail in Volume 18 of this series, large-scale deliveries of Soviet-made aircraft to Ethiopia were initiated in November 1977. By the end of that month, the Soviets delivered a total of 12 or 13 MiG-17Fs and two MiG-15UTIs (all from the stocks of the People's Democratic Republic of Yemen Air Force, PDRYAF, i.e. from South Yemen), 12 MiG-21MF fighter-bombers and 8 MiG-21UM conversion-trainers, 20 Mil Mi-8T assault helicopters and 6 brand-new Mil Mi-24 helicopter gunships.[121] The deliveries continued through December 1977, and thus by the end of that year Ethiopia received a total of 48 newly-built MiG-21bis' interceptors and up to a dozen MiG-21R reconnaissance fighters.

As far as is currently known, the first Soviet combat aircraft activated in Ethiopia were MiG-21UMs, which entered service with the re-established 33rd Squadron in order to convert all ex-F-86 pilots of the 1st and 2nd Squadrons EtAF. This process was supported by a group of Soviet advisors drawn from 160 Fighter Regiment (then based at Borisoglebsk AB), and 927 Fighter Regiment (Beryoza AB) of the Soviet air force, that arrived in Debre Zeit AB in December 1977, but also by Ethiopian pilots that converted to the type in the USSR.

Conversion to MiG-23s

The next large delivery for the EtAF took place in December 1977, when the air force received a total of 48 newly-built MiG-21bis' interceptors, at least four, perhaps up to eight MiG-21R reconnaissance fighters, the first batch out of 44 MiG-23BN fighter-bombers, and the first out of an eventual 30 Mil Mi-17 assault helicopters.

As indicated above, the first few EtAF pilots to undergo a conversion course on MiG-23s were already in the USSR as of November 1977, when they finished their training on MiG-21s. Almost immediately afterwards, they were flown to Lugovaya air base, where they met another group of Ethiopians: the team led by Lieutenant Colonel Gizaw Diriba, and including Captains Getachev Tekle-Giorgis, Nebiyu Abraha, and Kinfu Habtewold, and Lieutenants Tilahun Bogale, Tadesse Muluneh, Tadele Alemu, and Dessalegn Mebrate. At Lugovaya they joined a large number of student pilots from North Yemen, South Yemen, East Germany, Hungary, and Bulgaria, but also from Somalia. Surprisingly, a few

An Ethiopian pilot inside a cockpit of a MiG-23 while undergoing conversion to that type, at Lugovaya AB, in the USSR in 1978. (Pit Weinert Collection)

Lieutenant Colonel Teshale Zewdie de-briefing three student pilots after a training flight. In the background is the MiG-23UB serial number 1205. (EtAF via S. N.)

Group photo of the third group of Ethiopian ground personnel for MiG-23BNs: they completed their training in Ethiopia. (Pit Weinert Collection)

After acquiring 44 MiG-23BNs in 1978, Ethiopia continued placing orders for this variant: ten years later, more than 140 were acquired. This photograph offers a good look at the camouflage pattern, national markings (applied in four positions), and serial number. (Herve Dessallier via Albert Grandolini)

of the Somalis even spoke Amharic and proved very friendly to the Ethiopians. However, they left a few weeks later.

Flight training on the MiG-23 proved slightly easier than that on the MiG-21 because of better cockpit ergonomics. It was also not as restrictive: students were allowed to perform any aerobatics they desired. However, the Soviets were not willing to share any details about such advanced systems like the N23 navigational platform or the automatic bombing system – although the EtAF received MiG-23BNs equipped with such systems: the Ethiopians were told that they would be trained on such systems by Soviet advisors in Ethiopia.

By the time they graduated, five months later, the Ethiopians received exactly 20 hours of flight training on MiG-23s.

The eight pilots then returned home where they established a small squadron – supervised by two Soviet advisors. Eager to learn about the advanced systems of their new mounts, the Ethiopians then experienced their next disappointment: their Soviet advisors told them they never trained on these systems and knew nothing about them.

As soon as they started flying MiG-23BNs in Ethiopia, EtAF pilots found out that the fuel consumption charts were a way off from the actual fuel consumption of this variant. Not satisfied with useless explanations of their Soviet advisors, they decided to run test-flights from Debre Zeit to Dire Dawa at different altitudes and configurations and thus find out the exact details about fuel consumptions.

Five months after the first MiG-23BN unit was formed, five additional pilots joined it upon completing their training in the USSR. These were: Lieutenant Colonel Tigneh Habte-Giorgis, Lieutenant Colonel Teshale Zewdie, Major Mammo Gudeta, and Captains Asrat Tekalign and Takele Abebe.

With all the personnel and equipment in place, the Ethiopians made the decision to find out how to use the advanced systems of their aircraft. The two of most technically-minded pilots of the unit – Mammo Gudeta and Tilahun Bogale – eventually figured out how the systems in question worked using the simple 'trial and error' method. They concluded that the system enabled the pilot to enter the desired flight altitude, flight course, target coordinates and distance to target, and that this information was then linked with the auto-pilot, which could steer the aircraft throughout the flight. The Ethiopians developed a check-list for its use and taught all of their colleagues about the system.

Curiously, their Soviet advisors had heard about this check-list after some time, and requested them to hand it over. However, the Ethiopians denied its existence and kept it strictly for themselves. After some time, the Soviets ceased pushing this matter any further.

Ethiopian MiG-23BNs saw action in early April 1977, during the closing stages of the Ogaden War. Indeed, two were shot down by Somali air defences during the subsequent Operation Lash, which was a main counterinsurgency effort aimed at neutralizing the WSLF in north-eastern Ogaden, undertaken in early April 1978. Both pilots in question – Tadelle Alemu and Tadesse Mulluneh – ejected safely: Tadelle was captured and spent the next 10 years in a Somali prison, while Tadesse was recovered by an Ethiopian Mi-8 helicopter.

Fidel Castro (second from right) with a group of Ethiopian officials and Cuban officers during his visit to Debre Zeit AB in 1978. (EtAF via S. N.)

From the official standpoint of Havana, Cuban troops deployed in Ethiopia were protecting another popular revolution. Correspondingly, many Cuban officers and other ranks were firmly convinced they would be fulfilling their internationalist duty. Ethiopians went to quite some extent in order to convince them about their 'socialist' intentions and thus secure first Cuban, and then Soviet support. (Albert Grandolini Collection)

One of the ex-Soviet, ex-South Yemeni MiG-17s as seen at Dire Dawa, shortly after the end of the Ogaden War. Notable is the old, 'imperial' national insignia, and the RBK-250 CBU attached underwing. (Pit Weinert Collection)

A group of South Yemeni pilots (standing) with their Ethiopian hosts. (EtAF via S. N.)

Re-Equipment Process

The availability of large numbers of Soviet-made aircraft rendered EtAF's last two Canberra bombers surplus. Both were stored at Debre Zeit AB shortly after the end of Ogaden War and never flown again. A similar fate befell most F-5As and F-5Es: although Ethiopian technicians re-equipped all of the Tiger IIs that were still operational with hardpoints taken from MiG-21s – thus making them compatible with a wide range of Soviet-made arms – they saw only relatively little operational service afterwards. Nevertheless, some of the old F-86Fs and T-33As were retained in service well into 1979, until their crews completed their conversion training to the MiGs.

While some MiG-23BNs were flown in combat during the closing stages of the Ogaden War, most of them officially entered service only much later. Similarly, the first group of Ethiopian pilots for Mi-24s – including Berhane Meskel – was still undergoing their conversion training in the USSR when the Ogaden War ended.

Meanwhile, in order to buy time, but also because the EtAF flatly refused to accept MiG-17s and MiG-21MFs donated by the Soviets (Ethiopian pilots concluded both types for unsuitable for EtAF's purposes), these were operated by a group of foreign pilots that arrived at Debre Zeit in November 1977. The latter included up to a dozen of pilots of the People's Democratic Republic of Yemen (or 'South Yemen') Air Force, and a detachment from the Defesa Anti-Aérea y Fuerza Aérea Revolucionaria (Cuban Air Force and Air Defence Force). As far as is known, the Cubans and South Yemenis

were officially organized into the 4th Squadron and flew MiG-15UTIs, MiG-17fs and MiG-21MFs. The commander of this unit was a Cuban: Lieutenant Colonel Ruben Iterian.

Although the Cubans remained in Ethiopia for a number of years longer none of them ever flew any kind of combat sorties over Eritrea and Tigray: if at all, they only few additional combat sorties against Somalia and Somali insurgents that remained active in Ogaden.[122]

Overall, as of late 1977 and early 1978, the EtAF was organized as listed in Table 9 – with the observation that exact details of its organisational structure after the Soviet-style regiments were introduced, remains elusive to this day.

Considering the Ethiopians to be 'trained by imperialists' and 'in need of political re-education', the Soviets were particularly curious to change the 'American mindset' of EtAF's rank and file. Correspondingly, in 1978 Moscow offered Addis Ababa to train all future cadets in the USSR. At first look, the only drawback of this organization of training was the one year extra that the students had to spend in the Soviet Union learning the Russian language. Unsurprisingly, eager to make enormous cost savings, Addis Ababa accepted this offer, and the first group of Ethiopian students was sent for basic pilot training in the Soviet Union by the end of 1978.[123]

Expanded but Crippled Navy

The Ethiopian Navy, which used to total a mere 750 personnel during the last year of the Imperial era, was expanded to 4,750 and received a collection of torpedo boats (two Project 206E and two Project 206M), seven missile boats (Project 205), two frigates (Project 159),

Table 9: EtAF Order of Battle, late 1977/early 1978

Unit	Base	Equipment	Notes
1st Squadron	Asmara	MiG-21bis'	ex F-86F-unit; converting to MiG-21bis'
3rd Squadron	Dire Dawa	MiG-21bis'	ex T-28D- & B.17-unit; converting to MiG-21bi's
4th Squadron	Asmara	MiG-15UTI, MiG-17F, MiG-21MF	de-activated in 1975 or 1976; re-established as provisional squadron staffed by Cuban and South Yemeni personnel; later re-established and re-equipped with MiG-23BNs
5th Squadron "Tiger Squadron"	Debre Zeit	7-8 F-5A/B	CO Lt Col Techane Mesfin; Maj Berhanu Kebede took over during the Ogaden War; re-equipped with MiG-23BNs in 1979
9th Squadron "Tiger II" Squadron	Dire Dawa	5 F-5E	CO Lt Col Berhanu Wubneh; re-equipped with MiG-23BNs in 1979
14th Helicopter Squadron	Debre Zeit	3 SA.316B	CO unknown; expanded and partially re-equipped with Mi-8s in 1977-1978
21st Transport Squadron	Debre Zeit	20 C-47 2 C-54 9 C-119K	CO Lt Col Fanta Belay (later C-in-C EtAF); partially re-equipped with Antonov An-12s in early 1980s
31st Training Squadron	Dire Dawa	-	de-activated in 1973; formerly equipped with SAAB Safirs
32nd Training Squadron	Dire Dawa	MiG-21UM	re-activated as operational conversion unit for MiG-21
33rd Training Squadron	Asmara	T-33As & RT-33As	CO Lt Col Amha Desta operational conversion unit; re-deployed to Asmara during Ogaden War
44th Bomber Squadron	Debre Zeit	-	Disbanded in early 1977; re-established and re-equipped with MiG-23BNs in 1978

two landing ships (Project 771), one tanker, several minesweepers and other units, all provided by the Soviet Union and South Yemen. These ships were organized into five squadrons and operated from Asseb and Massawa. Furthermore, the Navy established its own commando unit and subsequently proved instrumental in moving Ethiopian troops and supplies along the Red Sea coast, although its operations were frequently impeded by technical problems and ships ill-suited to the task and climate circumstances. The older Project 205-type boats proved especially unable to withstand local weather conditions, and at least one of the Project 159 boats arrived lacking its flood-control instrumentation.[124]

Another factor that reduced the Navy's efficiency was disaffection with the Derg, because this failed to improve the living conditions of officers and other ranks. Thus, starting in the early 1980s, the

morale in the Navy dropped below all acceptable levels: while some men committed suicide, others defected and in November 1980 fled Massawa in a small boat. Mengistu reacted by ordering his security services to step-up monitoring of the service, instead of increasing food allowances and other benefits, and the climate in the service thus continued to deteriorate. When 11 Navy personnel were executed over suspicion of sympathies for the insurgents, dozens of sailors defected, while a crew of 21 defected with their patrol boat to the Yemeni port of Hodeida in January 1981 - although the government of the Yemen Arab Republic (also 'North Yemen' in the 1980s) returned the ship to Ethiopia only a month later. The security measures in the Navy subsequently became draconian: ships went to sea only in pairs, and always with an armed squad from the Army on board. Even then, a lieutenant managed to defect with a patrol boat by forcing 22 of his crew to jump overboard at gun point. Overall, by the mid-1980s, the Ethiopian Navy was hardly operational.[125]

Because most of them rapidly fell in disrepair, photographs of Soviet-made warships in service with the Ethiopian Navy remain extremely scarce. This Project 205 class missile-boat was photographed in the late 1980s. (Tom Cooper Collection)

To support the work of the navy, the EtAF acquired two Mil Mi-14 anti-submarine helicopters – including this example, serialled as 1681. Next to nothing is known about their operations during the 1980s, and it seems that none remained operational after the end of the Eritrean Liberation War. (EtAF via S. N.)

CHAPTER 5
COUNTEROFFENSIVE IN ERITREA

While the bulk of the Ethiopian military was committed against Somalia for most of 1977 and the first half of 1978, Eritrean insurgents continued their advance until nearly 80% of that province was controlled either by the ELF or the EPLF. Addis Ababa began reinforcing units of the People's Militia in September 1977, but these reinforcements proved only enough to prevent the fall of Asmara and Massawa.

Siege of Massawa

Late in September 1977, the Ethiopian Army attempted to break through the insurgent siege of Asmara. On the first day of this operation, a column supported by MBTs managed to dislodge a battalion of the ELA that controlled the road to Decamare, and to advance for 20 kilometres (12 miles) before stopping for the night. However, this halt enabled the EPLA to rush in reinforcements and establish additional blocking positions further down the road. Thus, on the next day, the insurgents not only stopped the further advance cold, but also outflanked it and caused sufficient casualties for the Ethiopians to retreat to Asmara.[126]

On 12 October 1977, a large convoy carrying supplies, and escorted by armour and elements of the 30th Infantry Battalion, moving from along the road to Asmara was ambushed while passing a narrow defile only 28 kilometres (18 miles) outside Massawa. In a carefully planned operation, the EPLA annihilated the protective force and destroyed or captured more than 300 vehicles. From that day onwards, the vital road connection was severed, and Asmara could only be re-supplied from the air. Following this success, the EPLA closed in on the crucial port, occupied all the hills around it and established a dense network of well-concealed and camouflaged positions.[127]

On 9 December 1977, the garrison of Massawa launched a strong counter-attack, supported by a battalion of recently acquired T-54 MBTs and other armoured vehicles, as well as EtAF air strikes, and naval artillery fire. However, well-protected in their trenches and bunkers, the insurgents suffered only minor casualties from this barrage. When the Ethiopian infantry advanced, the Eritreans slowly withdrew, enticing their enemy to advance into a valley until encircled from three sides. By counterattacking simultaneously from the front and both flanks, the insurgents collapsed the Ethiopian advance and forced survivors to retreat towards Massawa. On the next day, the EPLA captured the town of Dogali, the primary source of drinkable water for the crucial port. During that attack, they captured a total of 15 operational armoured vehicles, including several T-54s and BTR-60s.[128]

Although in an advantageous position, the EPLA subsequently proved unable to exploit the obvious disorganisation in the Ethiopian ranks. The primary reason for this was its own logistical problems: it took much too long to stockpile enough supplies from bases in the Sahel region. Thus, it was only on 20 December 1977, that the insurgents launched their attack on Massawa's airport. Despite constant air strikes by EtAF F-5s and T-33s – which frequently operated in pairs – this assault still managed to capture three quarters of the city and forced the garrison to retreat into the naval base, which was separated from the mainland by a 150 metre wide, and one meter deep, waterlogged area. Following an artillery barrage, the EPLA's infantry attempted to cross this obstacle on 23 December, but the Ethiopian firepower cut this assault to pieces. The insurgents subsequently admitted suffering 600 casualties during this battle. Indeed, the EPLA proved unable to do more than

Eritrean insurgents receiving a briefing prior to their next attack in 1977 or 1978. (Albert Grandolini Collection)

During the fighting for Dogali, in December 1977, the EPLA captured a total of 15 operational armoured vehicles, including T-54 MBTs and BTR-60 APCs. This T-54 and a BTR-60 were photographed just a few weeks later, on the Dogali Bridge, outside Masaw, while deployed against their former owners. (Albert Grandolini Collection)

continue the siege of the remaining garrison of Massawa for the next three months.[129]

Onslaught on Eritrea

The Ethiopian victory against Somalia, and continuous deliveries of additional Soviet equipment, eventually provided the Derg with ability to launch a counteroffensive into Eritrea in early 1978. For this operation, the National Revolutionary Operations Command established the II Revolutionary Army (SRA) with HQ in Mekelle, assigned no less than seven task forces with a total of 87,722 troops to it, and stockpiled enough supplies for six months of intensive operations. Following their recent victory in Ogaden, soldiers were in high spirits and looking forward to defeating not only the ELF and the EPLF, but also the TPLF and other insurgent groups in Tigray, while slogans like 'Mop up Tigray and annihilate Eritrea' were broadcasted by the Derg's propaganda apparatus.[130]

The plan for the relief of Asmara and Massawa envisaged a multi-pronged offensive. Task Forces 501, 502, 503 and 504 were concentrated in Gondar and Tigray Provinces: 501 was to advance from Gondar to Teseney; 502 from Shire to Badme and then Barentu, Agordat, and Keren; Task Force 503 was to follow along three separate axes of advance and converge on Asmara; while Task Force 504 was to remain in Tigray and conduct mop-up operations against local insurgent groups. Units already in Eritrea were significantly reinforced too: the garrison of Massawa formed the Task Force 505, the objective of which was to break the siege and advance in the direction of Asmara. The garrison of Asmara – re-organized as the Task Force 506 – was to launch its own offensive and simultaneously progress towards Mendefera, Decanbare, Massawa, and Keren. Finally, the garrison of Barentu was re-organized as the Task Force 507, while the EtAF re-deployed its remaining F-5Es and T-33s, and at least a squadron of MiG-21s to Mekelle airfield. Essentially, the overall objective of this offensive was to crush the main body of 'regular' insurgent forces around Asmara without letting them retreat into the Sahel region.[131]

To face this onslaught, the ELA and the EPLA each had about ten small brigades with a total of about 18,000 combatants.

The Ethiopian counteroffensive into Eritrea and Tigray was opened with air strikes and artillery barrages on the morning of 7 June 1978. The TPLF initially attempted to block the advance with a mere 1,000 combatants organized into eight companies, supported by eight battalions from ELA's 72nd, 75th and 77th Brigades. Initially, this force managed to halt the Task Force 503 in the Enticho and Shire area for a few days. Although claiming to have destroyed three tanks and killed over 500 enemy troops during a counterattack on Enticho on 13 June 1978, they found themselves exposed to ever more air strikes and artillery barrages, and were eventually forced to withdraw towards Eritrea.[132]

Elsewhere on 13 June 1978, the ELA and EPLA attempted to end the siege of Barentu with a coordinated assault on the positions of the Task Force 507. However, with this town positioned on high ground, they only found themselves exposed to the firepower of the reinforced garrison. The EPLA alone lost 150 combatants and one of its recently captured tanks, and the attack was repelled.

On 5 July 1978, Task Forces 501, 502 and 503 opened their advance into Eritrea. The first of these included the 3rd and 7th Infantry Divisions and several support battalions – for a total of 23,753 officers and other ranks – and easily recaptured Teseney just six days later, forcing the surviving ELA combatants to run over the border into Sudan. Task Force 503 recaptured Quala from the ELA on 21 July 1978, before continuing to Mendefera. It was in this area that Task Forces 503 and 506 imposed a major defeat upon the EPLA on 27 July 1978, thus securing the road connecting Addis Ababa and Asmara for the Derg.

Meanwhile, the garrison of Massawa – reinforced by the battle-hardened 10th Brigade – assaulted and quickly overran the EPLA's positions inside the city, and then re-took the local airport. The Ethiopian general offensive in Eritrea devastated the ELF: the ELA collapsed under the onslaught and dispersed into small groups.

The EPLA remained intact: on 28 July, it ordered its dangerously over-extended units to retreat from the Decamare area. Correspondingly, Task Forces 502 and 507 quickly reached Barentu and then seized Akordat on 9 August 1978. Nevertheless, the leadership of the EPLA was determined to continue the battle. In

Following the Ethiopian victory in the Ogaden War, Addis Ababa rapidly re-deployed large concentrations of its military into Eritrea. In high spirits and full of patriotism, thousands of young Ethiopians enthusiastically enlisted to fight for the defence of their nation. Most of them received only crash military training and were attached to different units of the Popular Militia – one of which is seen on this photograph from a military parade in Addis Ababa. (Albert Grandolini Collection)

Luckier and fitter Ethiopian volunteers were assigned to crack units of the army, where they were trained as commandos (seen in this photograph) or mountain infantry. They received more advanced training and better armament, and proved their mettle in combat. (Albert Grandolini Collection)

mid-August it concentrated 14,000 combatants of its regular units on three major defensive positions. One of these was in the Akordat area, and its purpose was to block the Ethiopian advance on Keren. The other consisted of a 15 kilometre (9 miles) long defensive position atop ridges north of Asmara: it blocked the roads connecting that city with Keren and with Massawa. The third consisted of an extended trench system surrounding the Massawa plain.

The Ethiopians concentrated their operations against the central of these positions by unleashing an assault by Task Force 506 on the hills north of Asmara. Although supported by up to two dozens of air strikes a day, massive artillery barrages, and tanks, all of these attacks were beaten back. By mid-September 1978, the EPLF claimed to have destroyed 21 tanks and captured 4 others, killed 12,500 and captured 2,000 Ethiopian soldiers in this area alone. Whether the

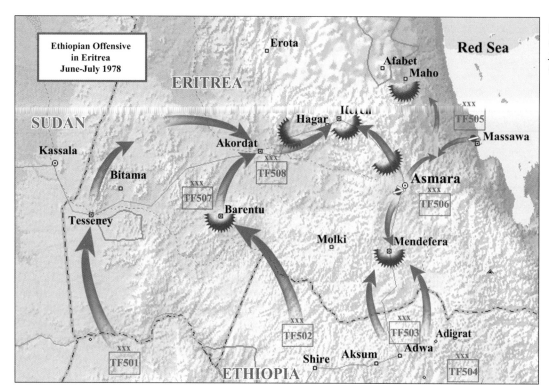

Map of major Ethiopian operations during the onslaught on Eritrea in June and July 1978. (Map by Tom Cooper)

Ethiopians really suffered such massive losses remains unclear, but it is certain that Addis Ababa stopped further attacks north of Asmara in late August 1978: after three months of nearly continuous advances, its troops were badly in need of rest, reorganisation and resupply.[133]

November 1978 Offensive

The Ethiopians re-launched their offensive on 17 November 1978, after re-organizing their main troop concentrations into the Task Force 506A and Task Force 506B. This contingent advanced along the road from Asmara in the direction of Keren. Simultaneously, the Task Force 505 opened an attack from Massawa in the direction of Asmara.

Right from the start of this operation, Addis Ababa released a number of reports pointing out that air strikes were instrumental in paving the way for success of its ground forces. Indeed, EtAF MiG-21s and MiG-23s bombed every single EPLA fixed position along the Asmara-Keren road that they could find, before these were assaulted by ground forces.

The EPLF's reports largely confirmed this, describing that the government forces had significantly improved their combined-arms tactics and reconnaissance: the air force targeted only carefully selected points in insurgent lines, Ethiopian mechanized columns attempted to outflank insurgent positions (as far as terrain permitted this), while keeping the defenders busy with diversionary attacks. Therefore, the Eritreans were left without a choice but to retreat in order to avoid encirclement.[134]

A good example of the Ethiopian tactics from this period was the fighting from the Adi-Yacob area, where an Ethiopian attack supported by about 60 armoured vehicles completely annihilated several platoons of an EPLA battalion and dispersed the survivors. Led by Omar Hassam Humed, commander of 8th Brigade, EPLA, the encircled Eritreans managed to break through, but meanwhile the Task Force 505 re-opened the Massawa-Asmara road on 22 November 1978.

One of the fiercest clashes of this campaign took place only days later, when Task Force 506A continued its advance along the Asmara-

A farmer in Filfil area, attempting to remove the fin of a Soviet-made FAB-250M-62 or FAB-500M-62 bomb from his field. Ethiopian fighter-bombers made prolific use of such general purpose bombs. (Photo by Dan Connell)

Intensive activity by the Ethiopian air force prompted the EPLA to make extensive use of all kinds of vegetation to conceal its positions. This radio station was skilfully hidden through a combination of branches from trees and bush. (Photo by Dan Connell)

Keren road until its vanguard – consisting of a mechanized brigade equipped with T-55s and BTR-60s – reached Elabered during the evening of 25 November 1978. As often in this mountainous part

The Ethiopian offensive along the Asmara-Keren road, in November 1978, was probably the last action for venerable F-86F Sabres in EtAF service. When this delegation of the Hungarian Air Force visited Debre Zeit, late in that year, at least six Sabres were still operational and flying, but most others – including the example with serial number 269, visible in the background - were already grounded and in the process of being replaced by MiG-23BNs. (Robert Szombati Collection)

Starting in 1977, the EPLA began deploying heavy weapons in combat – including such vehicles as this T-34/85 captured from Ethiopian forces. As far as can be determined, the tank was left in olive green overall, and devoid of any kind of markings. (Albert Grandolini Collection)

of Eritrea, the town was positioned in a basin surrounded by hills, and the EPLA put these features to good use by setting up a large ambush. The situation soon turned critical: all the radios with the Task Force 506A were lost, and thus the Task Force 506B was rushed to reinforce the unit that disappeared. Following a 36-hour-long intensive battle in which the EtAF played a crucial role by launching more than 70 CAS sorties, and dropped so many napalm- and high-explosive bombs that most of the valley of Elabered was filled with smoke – severely obstructing visibility and thus the ability of insurgent commanders to direct their forces – contact was re-established and the situation stabilized.[135]

Eventually, the insurgents were left without a choice but to evacuate Keren because, except for attacks by Task Force 506, the Ethiopians converged Task Forces 501 and 502 – which were meanwhile merged into the Task Force 508 – in the same direction, and these advanced rapidly from the direction of Akordat. Furthermore, Task Force 505 meanwhile made good progress along the road from Massawa to Afabet, and threatened to outflank insurgent units in the Keren area. Eventually, Task Force 508 entered the town on 27 November 1978.[136]

The 1st Nakfa Campaign

Understanding that the war was still far from over the Ethiopians almost immediately continued their operations. Task Forces 506 and 508 were ordered to advance on the last two EPLF-strongholds: Afabet and Nakfa. After successfully breaching the insurgent defences on the Mashalit pass, they quickly reached Afabet, but failed to prevent the EPLA from establishing a new defensive position defending Nakfa because the Task Force 506 suffered grievous casualties and first had to be completely reorganized.

With hindsight, it can be said that this was a crucial moment in the war: Ethiopian failure to capture the very epicentre of the EPLF enabled Eritreans to withdraw most of their regular forces into well-developed defensive positions, and to evacuate its political and logistic infra-structure and all of their sympathisers in time. The EPLF and the EPLA therefore not only remained intact, but also capable of launching local counterattacks – as was demonstrated by their eleven counterattacks on different outposts along the Asmara-Massawa road launched on 21 December 1978 – and then continuing their expansion. Indeed, on 22 February 1979, the insurgents captured the towns of Ghinda and Dongolo, located on this vital roadway, at least for a few hours. Furthermore, on 21 June,

the EPLA launched a similar attack on Decamare, and by mid-June it was once again free to operate in the countryside around Asmara.[137]

Meanwhile, in January 1979, Task Forces 506 and 508 launched a three-pronged offensive on Nakfa. All of their efforts ran into semi-circular defence lines that allowed Eritreans to enfilade assaulters from carefully camouflaged emplacements. Furthermore, the EPLA's main defence line was covered and concealed by logs, stones and sandbags, and thus well-protected from air strikes and artillery, and it included an uncovered ditch that attracted most of the Ethiopian attention. Thus, while during several nocturnal assaults, launched in the night from 14 to 15 January 1979, the Ethiopians managed – at great cost – to reach the unprotected ditch, they found that they had still failed to reach the main Eritrean defence line. Furthermore, although the two Ethiopian task forces greatly outnumbered the insurgents, the Department of Military Intelligence grossly overestimated the enemy although the EPLA had concentrated no fewer than four of its brigades, or a total of 5,000 combatants – the entire insurgent organisation totalled only eight brigades deployed on two different frontlines. On the other hand, what the Ethiopians failed to recognise in time was that the insurgents were far better equipped with heavy weapons (including up to 80 armoured vehicles), than expected.[138]

Despite all the Eritreans threw at them, the two Ethiopian task forces eventually punched through, forcing the EPLA to withdraw to a new defence line between Afabet and Nakfa. Perhaps more importantly, Task Force 505 increased the pressure by finally opening a new frontline in late January 1979 when a force spearheaded by the 29th Mechanized Brigade moved out of the small port of Mersa Gulbub along the coast of the Red Sea towards Alghena. In this fashion, the Ethiopians outflanked several Eritrean battalions concentrated in the Maemide area for the task of protecting the road from Mersa Gulbub to Nakfa.

Exploiting the moment of surprise, the Ethiopians took Alghena on 27 January 1979 and thus cut off the road connecting Nakfa with Sudan: only then did reconnaissance by EtAF aircraft discover a new, well concealed road constructed by the insurgents and connecting their stronghold with the northern neighbour. Furthermore, the EPLA rushed at least two battalions to the scene and these managed to stop the 29th Mechanized Brigade, even if this success came at the price of abandoning Mamide and several other positions in order to shorten the frontlines and free the necessary units.[139]

The Sahel Redoubt

Over the next two months, the Ethiopians launched several local attacks on the Nakfa front and along the Red Sea coast, but all of these failed to punch through – although by February 1979 they did reach positions from which their artillery was able to shell what was, de-facto, the EPLF's capital. Then, following another break for reorganisation and other preparations, the Derg unleashed a new offensive, this time simultaneously aiming to breach the Nakfa and the North Eastern Sahel Front of the EPLA.

Advancing from Afabet, Task Force 502 – then including 11 infantry battalions and the 1st Para-Commando Brigade, one artillery battalion and two BM-21 batteries – attacked a total of 12 insurgent battalions protecting their capital. Meanwhile, Task Forces 505A (including 6th, 8th, and 90th Infantry Brigades, 29th Mechanized Infantry Brigade, one tank and one artillery battalion), and 505B (including the 20th Nebelbal Brigade, 4th Para-Commando and 32nd Infantry Brigades, one tank-, one artillery- and one MRL-battalion) attacked in several places along the North Eastern Sahel Front, defended by three brigades of the EPLA, two of the ELA, and heavy weapons detachment from the 74th Brigade. Although supported by a large number of air strikes and pouring immense volumes of artillery fire into enemy lines, and despite heavy casualties, all of the attacks failed. To add salt to the injury, the insurgents did not confine themselves to pure defence, but also launched several counter-attacks.[140]

For all practical purposes, the conventional war between the Ethiopian military and the EPLA had reached a stalemate at this point in time, and no offensives launched by the Derg could change the

Well-armed and neatly uniformed, this unit of EPLA insurgents was photographed while cheering before going into the battle. Neither the ELF nor its military wing – ELA – ever managed to match the levels of organisation and sophistication in operations of the EPLF/EPLA. (Albert Grandolini Collection)

Amid reports about deployment of chemical weapons by the Ethiopian military, the EPLA equipped at last some of its combatants with makeshift gas-masks, starting in 1979. (Photo by Dan Connell)

situation. By shortening its front lines and drawing its enemy into terrain ideal for the defence, while retaining at least some limited land connection with Sudan, the insurgents followed a strategy that ensured their survival in the long term: through a combination of light infantry tactics and trench warfare in a mountainous terrain, they successfully equalled the quantitative advantages of their opponent, and left the Ethiopians to exhaust themselves in bloody futile attacks.

The EPLF did not sit idle during the relative respite that followed, but exploited this to end the presence of its forbearer and rival – the ELF/ELA. Although being closely allied since the Unity Agreement of 1977, the two movements were still frequently at odds, and this changed very little even when ELA units fought together with the EPLA on the Sahel redoubt in 1978 and 1979. Eventually, the ELA found itself entirely overshadowed by the stronger EPLA, and in August 1980 the EPLF opted to finish the rival. Unable to compete, completely outnumbered and out-gunned and already suffering from low morale, the ELA was left without a choice but to withdraw into Sudan. Behind the border, it gradually felt into decay and ultimately splintered into several groups, leaving the EPLF/EPLA – firmly entrenched in its Sahel redoubt – as the sole credible Eritrean independence movement.[141]

The so-called 'Sahel Redoubt' was protected by three defence lines, most of which consisted of positions skilfully constructed into the landscape. Thanks to their better knowledge of the local terrain, two or three insurgent bunkers as well-concealed as this one could up the attack of an entire battalion. (Photo by Dan Connell)

Poorly armed and lacking any kind of outside support, the insurgents of the WSLF still managed to bring much of Ogaden under their control in the aftermath of the Ogaden War. However, they stood no chance when facing the Cuban-supported I Revolutionary Army during the Operation Lash. (Albert Grandolini Collection)

The Last Derg Triumph

Although the Ogaden War ended in a clear-cut Ethiopian victory, several insurgent organisations remained active in south-eastern Ethiopia. The strongest of them was still the WSLF, which totalled around 12,000 combatants organized into nine divisions. This apparently impressive force was divided due to rivalries centred around different clans, which usually refused to help each other. Other movements fighting the Derg were the SALF, the Oromo Liberation Front (OLF), and the Islamic Front for the Liberation of Oromia (IFLO) – with the latter two at war with each other. Finally, the regular Somali National Army remained in control of a significant stretch of Ethiopian territory between the border towns of Ferfer and Mustahil, and Mogadishu continued providing at least some support to the SALF.

In August 1980, the I Revolutionary Army – including the 8th, 11th and 20th Infantry Division, the newly-formed 19th Mountain Infantry Division and commanded by Brigadier-General Demissie Gulto – opened the first of four stages of an offensive code-named Lash ('Ringworm'). Initially, the Ethiopians mopped up along the Ethiopian-Somali border, sealing all the major entry points into Ogaden. Operating in terrain far more suited for mobile warfare than in Eritrea, during Stages 2 and 3, multiple columns raided Ogaden, hunting down and eliminating insurgents. Due to the sheer size of this theatre of operations, this offensive proved a significant logistical challenge, and some of Ethiopian soldiers are known to have died of thirst, although EtAF deployed all of its helicopters in support of the involved ground units. Despite such difficulties, the SALF was annihilated, while the WSLF was left without a choice but to withdraw into Somalia.

Finally, Stage 4 – opened on 25 November 1980 with a three-pronged advance against Ferfer – resulted with the expulsion of the last Somali units out of Ethiopia and, ten days later, the I Revolutionary Army liberated the border town. Overall, Operation Lash proved a success and came at the – relatively – light cost of about 2,000 casualties.[142]

From the standpoint of the Ethiopian air force, the only major problem encountered at that time was the fact that the Eritrean insurgents acquired new weapons. For example, on 18 May 1981, they claimed a MiG-21 as shot down by SA-7s about 80 kilometres (50 miles) south of Asmara.

Meanwhile, the 18th Mountain Infantry Division (commanded by Lieutenant-Colonel Mardasa Lelisa) was deployed into Tigray after completing its one-year-long training. Beginning in August 1980, it cleared the Gondar-Shire road and then deployed elements of its 35th and 37th Brigades – supported by Mi-24 helicopter gunships of the EtAF – to destroy insurgent bases. In one rare application of the 'hearts and minds' strategy, Lelisa's units treated the local population well, and this helped them overrun most of training camps and arms depots without difficulties, in the period 13-23 February 1981.

Nevertheless, the TPLF survived: it dispersed its fighters and needled Ethiopians with numerous hit-and-run attacks. Logistical difficulties then prevented the Ethiopians from finishing the insurgency in the decisive moment: instead of continuing their advance, they were forced to withdraw into relatively few isolated strongholds, all of which then found themselves on the receiving end of additional assaults. Eventually, the Derg recalled all of the 18th Mountain Infantry Division and re-deployed it for protection of multiple vulnerable spots, in turn enabling the TPLF to regain the initiative.[143]

A group of Ethiopian pilots in front of one of the MiG-21bis' from the second batch of this variant to reach Ethiopia in the 1979-1980 period. By this time, most of them were combat veterans with dozens of attack sorties in their log-books. (EtAF via S. N.)

CHAPTER 6
RED STAR – RAISING AND FALLING

Following its large offensives in Ogaden and Tigray, the Derg felt free to search for an end to the war in Eritrea through a new, massive onslaught on the EPLF's Sahel redoubt. Correspondingly, ever bigger stocks of various supplies and ammunition were stockpiled in Gondar, Tigray and Eritrea during 1981. Furthermore, no less than 14 divisions of the Ethiopian military – including nearly 140,000 troops – were concentrated in these three provinces. They were to become the centrepiece of what was officially announced as the 'Red Star Multifaceted Revolutionary Campaign'.

Preparation of the Battlefield

The Red Star Campaign was supervised by a new commanding body, the Military Operations and Planning Command (MONPC), chaired by Mengistu Haile Mariam from a HQ in Asmara. Several of the divisions were raised and trained especially for this operation, although their training was drastically shortened in order for them to deploy on time. These were the 21st and 22nd Mountain Infantry Divisions and the 23rd and 24th Infantry Divisions. Other elements of the ground forces were reorganized too, and a new command-system introduced, centred around the Izz ('Command') in place of earlier task forces. The brunt of this offensive was to be carried by the commands code-named Wugaw ('Trash'), Nadew ('Destroy') and Mebrek ('Thunder'), elements of which were to assault the EPLF's Sahel redoubt. Two other commands, Meakalwi ('Central') and Mekit ('Shield') were to secure rear areas and conduct COIN operations in Tigray and Eritrea, respectively.

With units assigned to the Wuqaw, Nadew and Mebrek having the task of saturating and overwhelming the EPLA's defences by simultaneous attacks from multiple directions, they were also the strongest of the five commands. Each of these three commands included three infantry divisions and multiple support units, they totalled 66,749 officers and other ranks, 99 MBTs, 271 field guns and howitzers, and 48 BM-21s. The crack 18th Mountain Infantry

Division was kept in reserve. The overall Ethiopian order of battle for the Red Star Campaign is listed in Table 10.

The EtAF was to play a more important role than ever before. Not only did the air force MiG-21Rs fly dozens of reconnaissance missions – nearly a half of these by night – over insurgent-controlled territory, but it also deployed two squadrons equipped with MiG-21bis', two equipped with MiG-23BNs, and one equipped with Mi-24 helicopters in support. Most of the aircraft and helicopters in question were based at Asmara and Mekelle airfields, which were expanded and partially fortified, and the military sides of which received the status of 'air bases' under the control of the newly-established 3rd Wing.[144]

Furthermore, the EtAF replaced its old and worn-out C-119s with Antonov An-12B transports: these not only proved capable of hauling heavier loads, but were frequently used as makeshift-bombers during the Red Star Campaign: for this purpose, An-12s were usually loaded with bombs tied to pallets which were disgorged through the rear cargo door.

Aerial reconnaissance proved highly important for helping the MONPC to establish the precise locations of the three concentring and successive defence lines of the EPLA. Further intelligence about the insurgent organisation was provided by Teklai Gebre Mikael – a member of the Central Committee EPLF and Head of its Internal Security Department, who defected in 1980. However, the Ethiopians still lacked human intelligence sources within the EPLA. Correspondingly, they had to estimate on the basis of old information provided by Mikael and their reconnaissance photographs. One of their assessments was that the EPLA totalled between 20,000 and 25,000 combatants, organized into nine or ten brigades. These were supported by 15 MBTs and 14 other armoured vehicles, and 16 field artillery pieces organized into five specialized battalions. [145]

Contrary to earlier times, these estimates were understatements, because sources close to the insurgency later reported the EPLA's

An EtAF-pilot with his MiG-23BN around the time of the Operation Red Star. Notable is that he was still using a US-made helmet. (Pit Weinert Collection)

Towns controlled by insurgents were subjected to vicious air strikes of EtAF's fighter-bombers in preparation for the Red Star Campaign. This scene is from Badme following one of dozens of air strikes that hit the place in late 1981 and early 1982. (Photo by Dan Connell)

Newly-acquired An-12B transports of the EtAF played the crucial role in moving troops and supplies necessary for the Red Star Campaign to Mekelle, Asmara, and Massawa in early 1982. One such aircraft was claimed as shot down by EPLA SA-7 MANPADs on 14 January 1982. (Tom Cooper Collection)

strength at 27,000 troops – of which 5,000 were deployed on the North Eastern Sahel Front alone – supported by 150 armoured vehicles.[146] The reason for the insurgency having more fighters than the Ethiopians expected was that it now included around 3,000 TPLF combatants that withdrew from Tigray and were re-trained by more experienced Eritreans. Indeed, when an impeding Ethiopian onslaught became obvious, the EPLF's leadership expressed a special request of the TPLF's Central Committee to permit them to deploy these 3,000 combatants for the defence of the Sahel Redoubt. The Tigrayans agreed, and placed this force under temporary command of the EPLA.[147]

Perhaps more importantly, the EPLF became aware of the Red Star Campaign at least several weeks in advance, and even warned the international press about it in January 1982. The primary reason for this was that the Derg's propaganda made no secret about an upcoming offensive; secondary, that the preparations for an operation of this size were impossible to hide. Thirdly, the EPLF

human intelligence capabilities paid handsome dividends when it got hold of detailed plans for the operation.[148]

Indeed, the insurgents did much more than 'just' call their Tigrayan allies for support: instead, they launched two spoiling attacks, aimed at weakening the morale of Ethiopian troops before the start of the new offensive.

The Red Star Campaign was preceded by a full month of unprecedentedly intensive air strikes in which insurgent positions were subjected to extensive use of RBK-500 cluster-bomb units (CBUs) filled with incendiaries (like phosphorus) and ZAB-350 napalm bombs, while EtAF transports were used to help move many army troops. The EPLF attempted to hit back – and succeeded. On 14 January 1982, it used SA-7s again – this time to shoot down an Antonov An-12 transport near Asmara, killing all 73 on board.[149]

Only nine days later, at dawn of 23 January 1982, five EPLA battalions with around 2,500 troops suddenly attacked Asmara and successfully breached its defensive perimeter by overwhelming two separate positions. After assaulting the HQ of the 35th Mountain Infantry Brigade (18th Mountain Infantry Division),

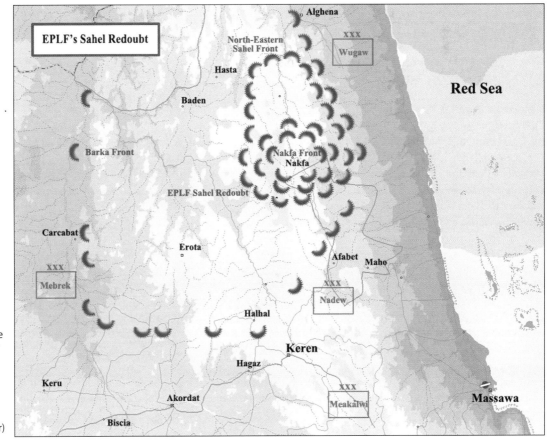

Map of northern Eritrea with the approximate area controlled by the EPLA, and the approximate positions of the three defence lines protecting the Sahel Redoubt – as around the time shortly before the Red Star Campaign. (Map by Tom Cooper)

Table 10: Ethiopian Army Order of Battle, Operation Red Star, February 1982

Unit	Commander	Notes
Wuqaz Izz	Brigadier General Aberra Abebe	21,581 troops
15th Infantry Division		
19th Mountain Infantry Division		
23rd Infantry Division		
Nadew Izz	Brigadier General Wibatu Tsegaye	20,801 troops
3rd Infantry Division	Colonel Teshager Yenam	
17th Infantry Division	Colonel Makonnen Wolde	
22nd Mountain Infantry Division		
Mebreq Izz	Briadier General Kumlachew Dejene	24,367 troops
2nd Infantry Division		
21st Mountain Infantry Division	Colonel Wubishet Mamo	
24th Infantry Division		
Mekit Izz	Colonel Abdulahi Umar	
6th Infantry Division		
14th Infantry Division		
Maekalwi Izz		
1st Infantry Division		presence uncertain
16th Infantry Division		presence uncertain
18th Mountain Infantry Division		reserve, under direct command of the MONPC

they also raided the military side of Asmara airfield, and claimed the destruction of seven fighter-bombers, two transport aircraft, and three helicopters.[150]

Another spoiling attack followed on 13 February 1982, and hit the 40th and 41st Brigades of the 19th Mountain Infantry Division, assigned to the Wuqaw Command. This time, the insurgents overran the main Ethiopian base, causing 1,244 casualties – more than a quarter of the total allocated manpower of these two brigades. The insurgents were forced to withdraw only when hit by severe air strikes, followed by an artillery barrage and a counterattack by the 39th Mountain Infantry Brigade.[151]

Demise of the 21st Mountain Infantry Division

Despite spoiling attacks by insurgents, the Red Star Campaign was launched by all three of the involved commands as scheduled on 15 February 1982. Divisions of the Mabreq command advanced along two main axes, and things went well for the massively reinforced 2nd Infantry Division as this attacked along the Keren-Asmat road and captured Hal Hal and Fil Fil, before taking Asmat.

However, the main attack of the Mebreq Command came from the Carcabat area in the form of the 21st Mountain and the 24th Infantry Divisions advancing across the plains separating the Barka River from the mountain ranges of the Sahel. The two units initially made good progress: the 21st took Kur during the morning of 16 February, while the 24th took several dominating peaks in this area. However, two days later, the 44th Brigade of the 21st Mountain – which failed to patrol the no-mans-land between itself and EPLA's positions – was hit by a violent artillery barrage, and then a series of counterattacks that forced it to retreat. Disaster struck when the EPLA captured the only water well under the control of that division – a crucial area in what was essentially a desert, yet defended by only one platoon. This turned the retreat into a rout, in which the 21st suffered extensive casualties both in combat and due to thirst. In

EPLA insurgents learned very quickly how to construct good fortifications in the rugged terrain of northern central Ethiopia, and perfected the tactics of defending these. This photograph shows a team armed with a Browning M2 heavy machine gun – captured from the Ethiopian Army. (Albert Grandolini Collection)

turn, the demise of this division dramatically exposed the flanks of the 2nd and 24th Infantry Divisions, and forced them to retreat back to their points of departure by 25 February 1982.

Map depicting opening phase of the Red Star Campaign, in February 1982. (Map by Tom Cooper)

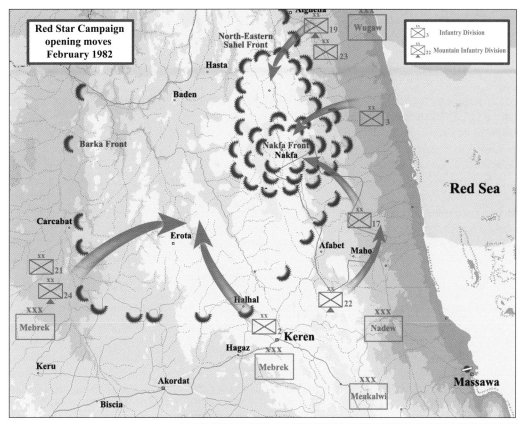

The MONPC than made a critical decision by stopping any further attempts on the Barka front, and used the units of the Mebreq Command to reinforce other fronts. Correspondingly, the 24th Infantry Division was assigned to the Nadew Command in late February, followed by the 2nd Infantry two weeks later. This drastic reduction of the number of axes of advance allowed the EPLA – which always kept the advantage of interior lines – to concentrate its manpower on the other fronts too. Still, worst was to follow: commander of the 21st Mountain Division, Colonel Wubishet Mamo, was declared primary culprit for this failure and executed in front of his troops; Mabreq Command was dissolved and replaced by a similar body, code-named the Manter Command ('Mop up').[152]

Thus, starting in late February 1982, the Wuqaw and, to a larger extent, the Nadew Command bore the brunt of the Red Star Campaign. Initially, everything went according to plan. On 15 February 1982, the 15th Infantry Division crossed the Sudanese border at Qarora and took the EPLA by surprise when it captured the 1,785 metre (5,856ft) high Mount Dambobiet at dawn the next day. With this, the insurgent connection to Sudan was lost. The EPLA launched a number of vicious counterattacks during the following days: while these failed to dislodge the Ethiopians from the dominating peak, they at least prevented them from bringing other important hills under their control. Eventually, the insurgents recaptured Mount Dambobiet only in March, and then by a multi-prong attack.[153]

Meanwhile, the Weqaw Command's two other divisions also met with initial successes. The 23rd Infantry took two EPLA bases near Alghena and then advanced toward Afchewa to cut the Alghena-Nakfa road, while the 19th Mountain captured several hills dominating the area southwest of Alghena, and then attacked in the direction of the Adobayah Pass. However, EPLA's resistance soon gained in strength and both Ethiopian units were finally stopped – despite receiving plentiful CAS from the EtAF.

On 18 February, the insurgents counter-attacked the 19th Mountain and caused it to give up all the gains of the previous three

As so often before and after, Ethiopian units involved in the Red Star Campaign of 1982 suffered their heaviest losses while attempting to overcome well-concealed and protected positions of EPLA insurgents. This bunker was partially dug in, and then covered by several layers of logs, rocks and earth. (Photo by Dan Connell)

days. Furthermore, on 5 March 1982 the EPLA outflanked the 23rd Infantry by exploiting gaps between it and the 3rd Infantry Division of the Nadew Command, and fell on its rear, forcing it to withdraw too.

Reinforced by the 21st, 93rd, and 104th Brigades re-deployed from Ogaden, the Wegaw Command resumed its offensive a week later, with the 23rd Infantry Division and half of the 19th Mountain Infantry Division, but both units battered themselves against insurgent positions they could not overcome. This attack was finally stopped on 23 March 1982. The 15th Infantry and the 19th Mountain Divisions did attempt to advance in the southern direction and thus to assist a general attack launched by the Nadew Command in the last days of that month, but without notable success.[154]

Bloody Hill 1702

The offensive of the Nadew Command was opened on 15 February 1982, with the 3rd and 17th Infantry Divisions advancing along what the Ethiopians assumed would be an unexpected axis, from Afabet towards Nakfa. Both units made a hook across the sandy plains separating the Den Den and the Kahul area, before turning to hit the EPLF's redoubt and sever the Aghena-Nakfa road. The third major unit of this command, the 22nd Mountain Infantry Division remained in the Afabet area to tie down EPLA forces there with diversionary attacks, but also to secure rear lines of communication.

The rapid advance of the two divisions did take the EPLA by surprise, and between 17 and 20 February the Ethiopians seized several critical heights, including Hills 1702, 1725, 1755, 1527, and 1590. The 9th Brigade of the 3rd Infantry Division, and the 19th and 84th Brigades of the 17th Infantry Division thus reached areas as close as a few kilometres from Nakfa.[155]

The crisis forced the insurgents to rush whatever reinforcements were available to this frontline – even if this meant weakening positions facing the Weqaw and Mabreq Commands. Even the EPLF's civil cadre was mobilized and armed *en masse* to face the Nadew Command's onslaught.[156]

On 23 February 1982, the EPLA had massed sufficient forces to launch a counterattack supported by tanks and artillery. Using a gap to outflank the enemy, the insurgents managed to push back the 3rd Infantry Division, which, to add insult to injury, was then heavily hit by an EtAF air strike too. Surprisingly enough, the Ethiopian units still retreated in good order.

Meanwhile, the EPLA re-directed its attention against the 19th Infantry Brigade of the 17th Infantry Division, which was defending Hill 1755. Once this was forced to withdraw, the nearby 84th and the 92nd Brigades had to do the same, because their flanks became exposed. Thus, the insurgents retook Hills 1755, 1702, and 1590 without much fighting, and while killing the commander of the 17th Infantry Division.

Determined to succeed, the MONPC reacted by releasing the 18th Mountain Infantry Division from reserve and allocate it to the Nadew Command. On 26 February, the fresh unit – reinforced by elements of the 3rd Division – launched a major attack, but the EPLA reacted with a quick counter-attack in the course of which it encircled the 36th Brigade and forced it to establish an all-round defensive perimeter. The encircled mountain infantrymen were eventually saved by an attack of the 38th Brigade, which allowed them to escape from this predicament. This action cost the 3rd

Two EPLA-insurgents waiting for their turn to take part in an assault. Notable are their plastic sandals: mass produced locally, they were worn by virtually all of the Eritrean combatants. (Photo by Dan Connell)

Commanders of an EPLA battalion briefing their fighters before the next battle. Machine-gunners in the foreground are proudly showing a typical mix of arms of Belgian, US, British and Soviet origin. (Albert Grandolini Collection)

Infantry Division its commanding officer, Colonel Teshager Yenam, who was killed in action.[157]

The Failure of Red Star

Despite the ultimate failure of the Nadew Command's advance, nearly all the subsequent Ethiopian efforts in the course of the Red Star Campaign were concentrated in this area. Correspondingly, the 2nd and 24th Infantry Divisions, and the 21st Mountain Infantry Division were re-deployed there, while exhausted units – like the 3rd Infantry Division – were withdrawn for quick reorganizations and some rest, before being thrown into the furnace again.

In early March, the 17th and 24th Infantry, and the 18th Mountain Infantry Divisions launched a major attempt to recover all of the important hills around Nakfa. The 17th took Hill 1702 on 3 March, but lost it just a day later, before it was replaced by the 24th, which made several attempts between 10 and 20 March. The slugfest between the two adversaries continued on 16 March, when the 2nd, 18th, 21st, and 22nd Divisions – supported by heavy air strikes, and also dozens of re-supply flights of EtAF's helicopters and transports – launched a new attempt. This was even supported by a fake para-drop, in the course of which transport aircraft dropped dummy parachutists behind EPLA positions to cause confusion. All the attempts failed, nevertheless, just like the nearly-suicidal assault on Hill 1702 by volunteers drawn from all units of the Nadew command. The last all-out attack took place during the last week of May and the first week of June, with the Weqaw Command attacking from the North, and the Nadew Command's 21st and 22nd Mountain Infantry, and the 24th Infantry divisions, advancing from Afabet along three different axes in an attempt to wrong-foot the EPLA. Nothing worked: the Red Star Campaign ended in early June 1982, by which time the Nadew Command's original three divisions had lost as up to one eighth of their troops killed in action.

Altogether the campaign cost the Ethiopians a staggering 37,136 casualties, including 1,074 officers. Much more than this, and in the words of Colonel Sereke-Berhan – future commander of the 3rd Infantry Division -

The Red Star Campaign was a turning point in the war in Eritrea. It bled and broke the morale of the army, which never fully regained its fighting spirit.'

Almost unsurprisingly, mutinies subsequently erupted in the 9th, 10th, and 93rd Infantry Brigades of the 3rd Infantry Division, soldiers demanding to be allowed some respite.

The EPLA's losses were severe too, with at least 3,600 combatants killed and up to 12,000 wounded. Although the insurgents inflicted

By the time of the Red Star Campaign, massive, sometimes days-long air raids by EtAF fighter-bombers on towns and villages controlled by the insurgency were a norm, and the EPLA did whatever was possible to bolster its air defences. Amongst weapons used for such purposes were old 40mm Bofors L/60s, famous from World War II – and captured from the Ethiopian military. (Albert Grandolini Collection)

Most terrain in northern central Eritrea is characterised by endless chains of rocky hills, with very few water sources. Correspondingly, water sources and distribution were often crucial for the outcome of fighting. Due to lack of roads, everything had to be carried by pack animals – and people. This rare still from a video is showing EPLF suppliers bringing water to a combat position high in the hills. (Adrien Fontanelaz Collection)

far higher losses on the enemy, their rate of loss was comparable. They emerged as victorious because they resisted the onslaught and retained most of their positions.

On the tactical level, EPLA insurgents reaped the benefits of the larger autonomy their high command allowed to its low-ranking officers, providing them with the ability to react far more quickly to developments on the battlefield than their Ethiopian counterparts. Furthermore, the coordination between different Ethiopian military branches was often insufficient: it took the artillery much too long to react to calls for help, and the chain of command was so complex that the EtAF – which, in theory, could deploy its superior firepower to devastating effect against advancing enemy infantry – was most of the time too late to react to Eritrean counterattacks.[158]

The Stealth Offensive

Considering the scope of the Ethiopian defeat during the Red Star Campaign, it might sound absurd that the Derg still came to the conclusion of launching another large-scale attack on the Sahel Redoubt early in 1983. However, that time the action was initiated in response to intelligence reports about an imminent EPLA offensive. Furthermore, drawing lessons from Red Star, the Ethiopians went to great lengths to maintain operational secrecy. So much so, they actually managed to take the insurgents by surprise – which is why the operation in question became known as the 'Stealth Offensive'.

In February 1983, the Nadew and Manter Commands – the former reinforced through the addition of the 15th Infantry- and 19th Mountain Divisions, and the 29th Mechanized Brigade from the Wuqaw Command – launched a three-pronged attack on the redoubt. Like the Red Star Campaign, the Ethiopians initially achieved significant advances. However, most of the gains were reversed by EPLA counterattacks in June 1983. Overall, after four months of protracted and largely fruitless battles, the Derg suffered the loss of another 17,648 casualties.[159]

At least as alarming was the fact that the Ethiopian military meanwhile proved unable to run successful COIN operations within areas under its nominal control. Attempts at 'hearts and minds' policy – including investment of more than US$ 100 million into infrastructure-rehabilitation projects, and a massive program for re-settlement of the rural population spent in Eritrea in 1981 alone, all proved insufficient to improve the living standards of the civilians. Local pro-government militias raised to keep insurgents away from Eritrean communities, and the violent repression constantly waged by the Derg security apparatus, all conspired to make occasional attempts to destroy the EPLF's clandestine infrastructure entirely ineffective. While attracting a lot less public attention than the ebb and flow of the conventional war, the Derg's inability to prevent its opponents form gaining ever more popular support proved spectacularly instrumental in its final demise.

CHAPTER 7
THE ROAD TO AFABET

While the EPLF spent most of 1981 and 1982 struggling to defend its Sahel redoubt against massive Ethiopian onslaughts, the TPLF exploited the situation to grow stronger. By 1984, the movement controlled most of the Tigray countryside, while government forces were confined to towns like Adigrat and Shire. Every movement of Ethiopian military convoys along local roads required heavy protection by the army and the air force. An attempt to counter the insurgency with the help of locally-recruited units – designated the Dragons – only enhanced the insurgent popularity, because

the troops in question became infamous for summary executions, looting and rape.

The TPLF continued maintaining its strong regular contingent in the Sahel redoubt until early 1985, by when close military cooperation had been established between the two movements. This relationship was beneficial for both groups: the TPLF could not afford for the Derg to destroy the EPLF, and thus free forces for large-scale operations in Tigray. The EPLF was well-aware of the value of TPLF's operations, because this diverted forces that could otherwise be deployed inside Eritrea – and also complicated the logistics of the II Revolutionary Army through constant harassment of supply convoys.[160]

However, this mutually beneficial collaboration was eventually overrun by a number of political factors because – despite their similar Marxist-Leninist backgrounds – the EPLF and the TPLF developed significant ideological differences in other arenas. For example, the TPLF's main goal was to end the traditional Amara monopoly on power in Ethiopia and reform the state into a federal system. The EPLF insisted on Eritrean independence above all, and saw the Ethiopians as foreign occupiers. While the TPLF's doctrine implied that various Eritrean ethnic groups were eligible for self-determination, this was an anathema for the EPLF, which insisted on overcoming traditional identities through creating a new generation of Eritrean citizens. Finally, the TPLF never felt comfortable with the role of being a junior partner in this relationship, and eventually it crossed an unwritten 'red line' of the EPLF through its support for creation of the Democratic Movement for the Liberation of Eritrea – a potential rival to the existing insurgency.

In mid-June 1985 the EPLF severed its ties to the TPLF and denied the movement the use of its territories and infrastructure. This had dramatic consequences for the Tigrayan insurgency because its only road connection with Sudan – the road also used by various NGOs to haul food for starvation-stricken population of Tigray – transited Eritrean-controlled territory. To reinforce its new point, the EPLA even burned 30 trucks carrying aid provided by the UN and other organisations. Left without a choice, the TPLF enlisted tens of thousands of local peasants to construct a new road connecting Tigray with Gederef in southern Sudan within a mere three months. In this fashion, the movement secured its own logistical artery.[161]

Otherwise, the only worry the Tigrayan insurgency experienced throughout all of the mid-1980s, was a COIN operation run by the 3rd, 16th, and 17th Infantry Divisions of the Ethiopian Army between April and August 1987. As so often before and after, this experienced only meagre success.

Fall of Tesseney

Following the end of the Red Star Campaign and the Stealth Offensive, the EPLA took nearly a year to recover its strength before launching several larger operations again. All of these targeted different units of the II Revolutionary Army. Headquartered in Asmara, the latter was the largest Ethiopian military command, controlling no less than 13 divisions and about a dozen other major units – more than twice as many units attached to the I Revolutionary Army in Ogaden (headquartered in Harer).

On 15 January 1984 the insurgents assaulted and captured the towns of Tesseney and Ali Ghidir, claiming to have inflicted 1,200 casualties on government forces. No 'hit-and-run' affair, this operation aimed to establish control over the second line of Ethiopian communications linking the Sahel redoubt to Sudan.

Only a week later, the insurgents struck in a completely different region – and attacked the positions of the Weqaw Command in Alghena area on 22 February. However, units of the 23rd Infantry Division – the only large formation attached to this command – were on alert. They not only repulsed this attack but inflicted heavy casualties on the EPLA. Undeterred, the insurgents reinforced their units, and assaulted Alghena one month later. In the course of the battle fought between 19 and 23 March, they mauled the Weqaw Command: this suffered not only a loss of 3,639 troops, but also arms and equipment worth US$ 21 million before the Eritreans

By mastering the art of moving rapidly over rugged terrain the EPLA frequently outmanoeuvred much more powerful – but slower – Ethiopian army units and attacked them from unexpected directions. Notable is the webbing worn by the fighter in front: this was locally produced using different materials – including Ethiopian army boot leather. (Photo by Dan Connell)

Although traditional Eritrean society was dominated by suppression of their rights, the exigencies of war had liberated women. By the mid-1980s, up to a third of Eritrean combatants were women, and there appeared to be no distinction between the sexes in the allocation of tasks: they were given to those capable of doing them. (Albert Grandolini Collection)

withdrew. With this, the EPLF was in control of a long portion of the coast of the Red Sea.[162]

When the EtAF hit back with additional air strikes on Naqfa, the insurgents claimed a MiG-23BN as shot down on 16 April 1984.

Acquisition of MiG-23ML Interceptors

The next to find itself on the receiving end of the EPLA's raids was the Ethiopian Air Force – which was undergoing a dramatic change around this time. As described earlier, when re-training Ethiopian pilots from F-86s to F-5As, and then to F-5Es in 1976, the Americans not only helped convert pilots and ground personnel from one type to the other, but also taught them how to fully exploit their new mounts and weapons in combat. In comparison, when re-training Ethiopian F-86 and F-5 pilots to MiG-21s, the Soviets provided only sub-standard conversion training within a heavily controlled environment that required extensive ground facilities not available in Ethiopia. In the Soviet air combat system of the time, a highly experienced pilot sat in a control centre and controlled the entire battle de-facto 'by remote control'. Pilots were either fed instruction via data-link to their displays, or were told by the ground control, via radio, at what flight level to operate, bearing to the target, what power to apply to their engines, when to engage and other similar instructions. Contrary to the Americans, the Soviets never trained Ethiopian pilots to operate independently from outside support. Subjects like complex aerial operations, battle formations, and low-level navigation were no part of their curriculum. In essence, Ethiopian pilots taught to fly in the USSR, could only take-off, make a circle around their air base, and land back at their base.

All of this was an anathema for Ethiopians who based their operations on decision-making by pilots themselves, and aggressive operations including low-level flying. Unsurprisingly, as soon as the first group of their personnel returned from training in the USSR, Ethiopians were deeply disappointed. However, because their homeland found itself on the receiving end of multiple aggressions and was thus in great need of help, they did not complain. Over the next few years, the situation was relatively good: the EtAF was pleased by the MiG-21 and the ease with which this type was kept operational. Nevertheless, Ethiopian pilots did not take long to find out about multiple weaknesses of the type. Foremost amongst these was its short range – especially if carrying any significant amounts of weaponry – and comparably primitive navigational and attack systems. Concerned about the threat from the Somali air force that was re-built with some support from the People's Republic of China and Pakistan, in 1983 the EtAF requested deliveries of more advanced aircraft and Moscow agreed to sell MiG-23ML interceptors.

Once again, a number of senior EtAF pilots – between them Berhanu Wubneh, Mesfin Haile, Hatesion Hadgu and Bezabih Petros – travelled to the USSR for a conversion course. However, while referred to as a 'higher education' by the Soviets, this course proved a major disappointment. Major-General Ashenafi Gebre Tsadik later recalled:

On arrival in Lugovaya our pilots instantly noticed that Soviet instructors were not good at all. They had next to no operational experience while expecting their foreign trainees to qualify as instructor pilots while having a total of only 150 hours in their log-books. For all practical reasons, they were doing the same like they did with our students that underwent conversion training on MiG-21s before. A number of huge arguments developed between us and the Soviets. It was only then that we understood

In 1985, the EtAF received the first out of an eventual 18 MiG-23MLs. Originally acquired to counter the re-built Somali air force, but also certain threats from Sudan, these interceptors were eventually foremost used for ground attacks. This photograph is showing a group of pilots from 10th Squadron, and one of their mounts (serial 1809). (EtAF via S. N.)

why the Somalis lost as badly as they did in course of air combats during the Ogaden War. Their training was really bad. As the arguments continued, Habtesion Hadgu even had to leave the program …[163]

Overcoming all the problems, Ethiopian air force eventually mastered the MiG-23ML, and in 1985 established its 10th Squadron, equipped with a total of 18 aircraft of this variant.

Re-Establishment of Own Training Facilities

Nevertheless, following all the negative experiences from training in the USSR, the EtAF drew the conclusion that it had to re-start training its own personnel, and then do so on the basis of what it learned in the USA, and this despite replacing its faithful F-5s by Soviet-made MiGs. To even more anger from the Soviets, the Ethiopians thus not only introduced the tactics of operating their MiGs in combat as if these were US-made aircraft, but also in re-opening its own educational facilities.

Because all available training aircraft – like the T-28s and T-33s – had been out of service for several years, Addis Ababa was forced to buy new aircraft types. The choice fell on Italian-made SIAI Marchetti SF.260TPs, and Czechoslovak-made Aero L-39 Albatross. From 1984, all the trainees returning from the USSR were put through a training course on SF.260s and L-39s before being declared qualified for combat operations. Similarly, all the new student pilots underwent courses on SF.260s, L-39s, then F-5Bs and MiG-21UMs, based on the old curriculum that saw the use of T-28s and T-33s in earlier times.

Overall, for most of the 1980s, the EtAF was in a rather awkward position: while acquiring ever more Soviet-made equipment, it kept not only the organizational structure, but also training methods, doctrine and tactics inherited during the times it was receiving US support.

There was only one exception to this rule – but then one with far-reaching consequences for many officers and other ranks serving with the EtAF in the 1980s. Namely, while the air force continued applying US tactics in almost everything it did, the Derg modified the Ethiopian COIN strategy. Its new approach involved forcible displacement of much of the population into 'protected villages', followed by military offensives against economic assets remaining outside government-controlled areas, and 'supported' by air raids against major urban areas under insurgent control – always flown on direct orders from the top political leadership. This policy resulted in the war in Eritrea being characterised by massive Ethiopian ground offensives and atrocities against the local

One of about a dozen of SF.260s acquired by Ethiopia starting in 1984. All were painted in silver-grey overall, and had their engine cowlings painted in dark green. (Pit Weinert)

Ethiopian instructors and their students with one of 17 L-39Cs (serial number 1708) acquired starting in 1985. (Pit Weinert Collection)

population. This not only further antagonised the Eritreans, but also caused significant problems within the EtAF. Dissent spread within the air force during the early 1980s, because many of its pilots questioned the validity of attacks on clearly civilian objectives. Nevertheless, the Derg remained insistent and continued issuing such orders – with the result that most of the surviving EtAF pilots and officers experienced incredible problems with the authorities once Mengistu's regime was toppled from power in 1991. This is the primary reason why even today, although never meddling in politics as much as Army's officers did, even those Ethiopian pilots that are long since retired still remain extremely reluctant to speak openly about their careers with the air force.

Sale of Remaining F-5s

Around the same time, the EtAF made the decision to sell its remaining 4 F-5Es, 11 F-5As, 1 F-5B and 1 RF-5A: seven years since the USA stopped its support for Addis Ababa, the air force was critically short on spares for these, while the aircraft were in need of major overhauls – for which there was no time. On the contrary: with many air forces around the world flying the type, a sale of F-5s was promising to bring some badly needed hard-currency. Correspondingly, in 1984, Addis Ababa put the F-5s up for sale, and announced this in the public.

The first to show interest was the government of Thailand. However, the experts of the Royal Thai Air Force found the Ethiopian F-5s in such terrible condition that they refused to buy them. In an attempt to 'remove them from the market', the Central Intelligence Agency (CIA) of the USA then offered to buy all the aircraft at a price of US$ 7 million. It was in the course of related negotiations that the officials in Addis Ababa were contacted by an Israeli middleman who offered them no less than US$ 68 million for four F-5Es alone. Surprised, but in need of cash, the Derg accepted and – after receiving half the payment up front – delivered the aircraft in question, by ship, from Assab to Bandar Abbas in Iran. Their actual customer was the government of the Islamic Republic of Iran, itself meanwhile under a US-imposed arms embargo, but fighting a bitter war against Iraq and badly in need of replacements.

A team of technicians of the Islamic Republic of Iran Air Force (IRIAF) arrived at Debre Zeit to inspect the four Tiger IIs, and found them to be in nearly unacceptable condition. While having only 497 hours of flying time on airframe on average, they suffered terribly from continuous exposure to the elements; all lacked their 20mm Colt M39 cannons; nearly all avionics were torn out, and technical documentation was missing. Unsurprisingly, the Iranians refused to accept the aircraft. Nevertheless, negotiations were continued and Tehran eventually came to the decision to buy not only the four F-5Es, but also 11 F-5As and the nose of the single 1 RF-5A for the US$ 34 million already transferred to Ethiopia. The aircraft in question were delivered to Iran in several batches: the F-5As in one shipment in 1985 and the other in 1987, while the last Ethiopian F-5Es reached Iran only in late 1989.[164]

Meanwhile, highly satisfied with the type, the EtAF continued placing orders for additional batches of MiG-23BNs. Until 1989, more than 140 aircraft of this variant were acquired, together with at least 9 MiG-23UB two-seat conversion trainers: they were operated by at least four squadrons, although it has to be kept in mind that nearly a third of the fleet was almost permanently unavailable: the aircraft in question were undergoing periodic overhauls in the USSR.

Despite Moscow's refusals to help in regards to spare parts and maintenance facilities, the Ethiopians continued their concerted efforts to establish a domestic capability to overhaul their MiGs. Coupled with relatively light losses during the war in Eritrea, this gradually resulted in increasing availability of MiG-21s and MiG-

EtAF F-5E serial number 419, as seen at Debre Zeit in 1978. Four of these aircraft were sold to Iran in 1985, but precise details about only two of them are known. The R1179, EtAF serial 418, became IRIAF's 3-7319, while R1182, EtAF serial 421, became 3-7320. (Pit Weinert Collection)

A group of EtAF pilots proudly posing with one of their mounts, parked inside a blast pen at Asmara AB. Notable is that all of them were using US-made helmets. Because of the general disorder in the Ethiopian Army, beginning in the mid-1980s, the EtAF was almost single-handedly preventing the EPLF from expelling Ethiopians out of all of Eritrea. (EtAF via S. N.)

23s during the late 1980s. Contrary to other Ethiopian military services, the EtAF was thus growing ever more powerful.

Raids on Asmara Airport

Finding itself on the receiving end of ever more air strikes the EPLF decided to act. Lacking other means to hit back, but in possession of superior intelligence-gathering capabilities in comparison to the Ethiopian military – which, reportedly, included presence of 'spies' in the EtAF – the insurgents became well-aware of deficiencies in the security of Asmara Air Base. Namely, this installation lacked blast pens for combat aircraft, and was only protected by the 15th Veteran Brigade – a second-rate unit. Furthermore, built-up areas close to the airport provided plentiful avenues of approach for any attackers.

Hence, at 2330hrs local time on 20 May 1984, 16 EPLA sappers breached the perimeter and entered the base. Within only 18 minutes, they destroyed eight EtAF aircraft: six MiG-23BNs and two helicopters. Two other MiG-23BNs, five MiG-21bis' and one transport aircraft were damaged. To add salt to the injury, the insurgents also claimed the destruction of two Ilyushin Il-38 maritime patrol aircraft of the Soviet Naval Aviation, forward deployed at Asmara.

While the Soviets subsequently ceased basing their aircraft on air bases in Eritrea, the local Ethiopian garrison learned very little. On 14 January 1986, another EPLA commando group infiltrated the Asmara Air Base – this time taking a B-10 recoilless rifle and several RPG-7 launchers with it. Before they disappeared in the night, the

Traces of heavy bombardment: wreck of a Soviet-made FAB-500M62 bomb that failed to explode during one of many air strikes on the Badme area, in December 1984. (Tom Cooper Collection)

Time and again, the EPLA attempted to move its artillery closer to the crucial Asmara airport: for this purpose it heavily camouflaged its artillery pieces, making their detection from the air exceptionally problematic. (Photo by Dan Connell)

Eritreans destroyed one, and damaged five MiG-21s, and set on fire the ammunition and fuel dumps.[165]

Operation Red Sea

Meanwhile, on 5 July 1985 the EPLA launched a major offensive against Barentu, which was defended by two brigades of the 15th Infantry Division, supported by one tank, and one commando battalion. This operation began with diversionary attacks at dusk against forward positions 35 kilometres (16 miles) outside the town to draw the garrison reserves out. The units deployed to protect the town had been recently reduced, and the EPLF knew it. A full EPLA

Living conditions on the frontlines of the Eritrean Liberation War ranged between austere and harsh. Not only that water was always a luxury, but combatants often spent months entrenched barely 50 metres away from each other. This group of EPLA regulars gathered around a machine gun team: their emplacements were often focal points of the fighting. (Albert Grandolini Collection)

Ethiopian UH-1H Hueys saw some of their last action during Operation Bahra Nagash in October 1985, when they were used in support of the 102nd Airborne Division. (EtAF via S. N.)

heavy brigade, well-equipped with support weapons and tanks, then launched its own assault from another direction. Despite their well-dug-in entrenchments, and good artillery support provided by two batteries each of D-30 howitzers, 76mm field guns and ZU-23 anti-aircraft cannons, the garrison was overwhelmed within only 24 hours.

The EtAF proved unable to throw its weight into the battle due to a heavy cloud cover, while the Army immediately rushed reinforcements from Agordat. However, deployed in piece-meal fashion, several of these – notably the 8th and the 106th Infantry Brigades – were ambushed and suffered extensive casualties. Unsurprisingly, yet prematurely, the EPLF propaganda subsequently claimed that the movement achieved a decisive victory in this war.[166]

As eager to retake Barentu as the EPLF was determined to hold it, the Derg once again deployed large reinforcements to Eritrea during July 1985. These even included 1,295 cadets from different military schools and commands. Code-named Operation Red Sea, this offensive included the 2nd Mechanized Division, four infantry divisions, and two independent mechanized brigades recently re-equipped with Soviet-made T-62 MBTs.[167]

This concentration of mechanized forces paid handsome dividends because, in contrast with the maze of valleys high in the Sahel, the corner formed by the border of Sudan and the Red Sea is dominated by barren plains – which are an excellent ground for mechanized warfare. The offensive began in mid-August 1985 and proved a resounding success. Although supported by 13 T-55s and 12 artillery pieces captured during earlier battles, the EPLA collapsed and ran away. Barentu was re-captured on 24 August, followed by Tesseney two days later. As usual, precise casualty figures for the EPLA remain unknown, but might have reached at least half of the 4,000 claimed by Addis Ababa.[168]

Operation Bahra Nagash

The success of Operation Red Sea enticed Mengistu Haile Mariam to order another offensive against the Sahel redoubt – code-named Operation Bahra Nagash. Addis Ababa issued numerous requests to Moscow for speedy delivery of vast amounts of supplies, and enough new combat helicopters to equip two squadrons, while the Army made the decision to deploy its recently established 102nd Airborne Division for large-scale airborne operations in EPLF-controlled territory. The rest of the plan for this operation followed the usual pattern, in the form of multi-pronged attacks. The Manter

Command (including 3rd Infantry and the 18th Mountain Infantry Divisions with 10,842 troops) was to advance from Agordat in the general direction of Zara, while the Nadew Command (19th and 22nd Mountain Infantry Divisions, and the 27th Mechanized Brigade) were to assault the Nakfa Front. A third, separate force – consisting of the 2nd Mechanized Division, reinforced by the 8th and 89th Infantry Brigades – was to advance from Kerkebet towards Nakfa.

However, the main blow was to be delivered by the newly-created Barged (Open Forcefully) Command. By far the strongest of all involved, the Barged Command included the re-established 21st Mountain Infantry Division, the 23rd Infantry and the 102nd Airborne Divisions, and the 16th and 29th Mechanized Brigades for a total of 17,081 officers and other ranks.

To achieve an element of surprise, this command planned to have the troops of the 102nd Airborne deployed by helicopters to the hills dominating Algena. These would then be reinforced through an amphibious landing of reinforcements. Once they had mopped-up the area, units of the Barged Command were then to advance along the Algena - Nakfa road.

Operation Bahra Nagash began on 10 October 1985, but was marred by numerous logistical problems right from the start. The Navy failed to ship the pre-arranged number of troops because of technical problems on numerous of its ships.[169] Similarly, the EtAF lacked helicopters to deploy all the necessary troops of the 102nd Airborne to their landing zones within the required period of time. Consequently, most of the troops of this division travelled to Algena by trucks.

While the Barged Command managed to take the town, all the above-mentioned problems caused such postponements that the EPLA was not taken by surprise. On the contrary, the insurgents quickly identified the threat and rushed reinforcements into the combat zone. Unsurprisingly, the Ethiopian advance soon stalled along the road to Nakfa – and the situation did not improve the least when units of the Nadew Command failed to make any significant progress.

After two weeks of stalemate, the Ethiopians decided to change their main axis of advance. The 102nd Airborne was re-assigned to the Nadew Command and on 12 August 1985 launched a large night assault, supported by a massive artillery barrage. Nevertheless, exploiting their advantage of interior lines, the EPLA deployed reinforcements to this frontline and stalled this advance in the usual fashion: through frequent ambushes and repeated counterattacks into the flanks of Ethiopian advance. Eventually, the Derg was forced

EtAF Mi-24s flew dozens of CAS sorties in support of the Operation Bahra Nagash and their attacks with unguided rockets were often decisive in the outcome of clashes on the ground. Ethiopia eventually acquired at least 24 helicopter gunships of this variant. (EtAF via S. N.)

By 1985 Mi-8s and Mi-17s completely replaced the remaining UH-1Hs of the EtAF. Contrary to the practice in some other air forces, they were foremost used for transport, sometimes for assault, and rarely armed for attack purposes. (EtAF via S.N.)

to suspend this offensive. By the end of August 1985, the Ethiopians suffered 14,442 casualties – including 3,545 killed in action.

Almost immediately, the EPLF launched its counterattack, aiming to hit the centre of the Manter Command in the Halal area. This move was threatening enough to compel the Ethiopians to rush the 22nd Mountain Infantry Division from the Nadew Command to help repulse the insurgents. When this proved insufficient, the 102nd Airborne was re-deployed too, and this managed to finally stabilize the frontlines.

The failure of large-scale offensives against the Sahel redoubt, and immense losses suffered by the Ethiopian military (between 1977 and 1986, the Ethiopians suffered staggering 196,944 casualties in Eritrea) took their toll on morale and discipline. Not permitted to return home 'until the ultimate victory' – or, more realistically until their death in battle – Ethiopians lost the will to continue the war. Indeed, even the Derg gave up trying. Operation Bahra Nagash was thus not only the last attempt to crush the EPLF, but also the moment Ethiopia lost the strategic initiative in the war.

Self-Destruction of the Nadew Command

The insurgency maintained the initiative by launching numerous operations of limited scale inside Ethiopian-controlled areas in 1986 and 1987. The II Revolutionary Army – reorganized into four commands (Barged, Nadew, Maket and Manter) in November 1985 – reacted by establishing new outposts and running regular sweeps, but without any notable success. Correspondingly, by May 1986, the EPLA managed to deploy its artillery near Massawa and shell not only military positions around the city, but also the harbour, blowing up fuel tanks in the process. The road connecting Massawa with Asmara once again became vulnerable to repeated ambushes. Under pressure from multiple sides, the Barged Command was forced to evacuate Algena in August 1986 and thus the ELPF was once again in control of the coast between Sudan and Massawa. During the first half of 1987, the Eritrean insurgents reportedly launched 84 operations against enemy troops, inflicting up to 4,300 casualties. By August 1987, they ran routine operations in the vicinity of Asmara, and even areas previously considered as secure were no longer safe. A supply convoy underway along the road from Asmara to Keren was attacked for the first time since 1977 and lost 18 trucks. In October 1987, another convoy lost 34 trucks in an ambush on the Asmara-Decamare road.[170]

Nevertheless, the Ethiopian military position in Eritrea remained imposing. Indeed, as of early 1987, the Nadew Command – meanwhile commanded by Major-General Tariku Ayne, an able

and popular officer – was the strongest within the II Revolutionary Army: it included the 19th, 21st and 22nd Mountain Infantry Divisions, the crack 29th Mechanized Brigade, and an artillery brigade. Altogether these units had 83 MBTs, 15 M-46 cannons, 35 D-30 howitzers and 10 BM-21s. Furthermore, this command was in control of the logistical base in Afabet, which was also the only spot in this part of Eritrea with sufficient water resources to keep such a large force supplied, and a total of 165 kilometres (102 miles) of frontline from the Red Sea to the Hadai Valley (most of this over very rugged terrain).[171]

The weakest spot in the Nadew Command was the 22nd Mountain Infantry Division, which held the part of the front anchored on the Red Sea coast. Aside from the usual grievances caused by the lack of rotation and supplies, the troops of this unit were also unsettled by the rivalries between their commander, Colonel Girma Teferi, his political commissar, Captain Sirak Workneh, and Workneh's replacement, Captain Fekadu Alemu. This rivalry had a catastrophic effect on the entire chain of command, resulting in a unit that was split into two – and this from its high-ranking officers down to the most junior soldiers. The net result was the collapse of discipline: as the number of insubordinations increased – especially within the 502nd and 503rd Battalions of the 50th Mountain Infantry Brigade – the Commander of the Nadew Command felt forced to intervene. However, his attempt to reinforce discipline only had detrimental effects. Not only several Military Security officers, but also radio operators of the 22nd Mountain Infantry Division defected to the Eritrean side as result. The EPLF thus found itself in possession of extremely detailed intelligence about an Ethiopian division – including its radio codes. Worst of all: responsible Ethiopian officers completely failed to react to this obvious security breach. They neither ordered a change in radio codes, nor any kind of modifications of existing positions.[172]

Unsurprisingly, always keen to exploit an opportunity, the insurgents quickly mobilized five infantry brigades and four heavy-weapons-battalions from their 74th Division and prepared an attack on the 22nd Mountain Infantry Division.

This began at 0400hrs in the morning of 8 December 1987 with a large-scale infantry assault. Almost immediately, this broke into Ethiopian defence lines and, by the next morning, resulted in destruction of Divisional headquarters. As the battle turned into a rout, the EPLA launched an advance of 20 to 30 kilometres (12-18 miles) into Ethiopian-controlled territory before the Nadew Command managed to re-deploy the 19th Mountain Infantry Division and the 45th Brigade of the 21st Mountain Infantry Division into the crisis zone. Supported by intensive air strikes of the EtAF, these managed to stop the insurgent advance.

Nevertheless, the defeat was severe: the Nadew Command lost 1,388 soldiers (including 482 killed, 291 wounded, and 615 missing in action). The MONPC was left without a choice but to withdraw the battered remnants of the 22nd Mountain Infantry Division from the frontlines and replace it by a second-rate unit, the 14th Infantry Division. Worst still, an infuriated Mengistu Haile Mariam flew to Asmara and, after a short but terse meeting with notoriously outspoken Major-General Tariku Ayne, had him executed on 15 February 1988. Similarly, the commander of the Mekit Command, Brigadier General Kebede Gashe, was demoted to the rank of a private.[173]

Even then, the mauling of the 22nd Mountain Infantry Division and the purge of top Ethiopian officers in Eritrea was only the first step in the tragedy that befell the Nadew Command. The next step occurred when Mengistu appointed new officers in charge: Colonel Getaneh Haile took over from Ayne, but for reasons of security, both commanders of the 14th Infantry and the 19th Mountain Infantry Divisions obeyed his orders only reluctantly – because both of them were Colonels too. Worst still, because these two units were at odds with each other, they failed to fill a four-kilometres (2.5 miles) wide gap separating them.

Of course, it did not take long for related news to reach the EPLF, the commanders of which found the Nadew Command – meanwhile down to 15,223 troops and thus the weakest of all four Ethiopian commands in Eritrea – a very tempting target. Through the last weeks of 1987 and into early 1988, the insurgents thus began preparing a multi-pronged offensive with intention of destroying this force.[174]

Table 11: Ethiopian and Eritrean Units of the Battle of Afabet, 17-19 March 1988

Units	Commanders
II Revolutionary Army (Ethiopia)	Brigadier-General Wubetu Tsegaye
Nadew Izz	Colonel Getaneh Haile
• 14th Infantry Division	Colonel Teshome Wolde Senbet
• 19th Mountain Infantry Division	Colonel Admassu Makonnen
• 21st Mountain Infantry Division	unknown
• 29th Mechanized Infantry Brigade	unknown
EPLA	
Nakfa Front	Mesfin Hogos
• 61st Division	Ali Ibrahim
• 70th Division	Philipos Wolde Yohannes
• 85th Division	Gebre Egziabher Andemariam
• 74th Heavy Weapons Division	unknown

Demise of the 29th Mechanized Brigade

For the operation ahead, the EPLAF mobilised three of its divisions and the entire 74th Heavy Weapons Division (for an overview of involved Ethiopian and Eritrean units see Table 11). Related preparations were made in utmost secrecy: not only that the commanders of involved units were informed about their tasks only

The EPLA always carefully reconnoitred every position of the Ethiopian army. This photograph shows a small town surrounded by significant fortifications in the Hedai Valley. (Albert Grandolini Collection)

The longer the war in Eritrea lasted, and the more casualties the Ethiopian military suffered, the less support the Derg enjoyed from the population. Opportunities to take photographs like this one, showing a T-55 MBT passing a cheering crowd of civilians, became extremely rare through the mid-1980s. (Tom Cooper Collection)

shortly before going into action, but the insurgents went as far as to organize a soccer tournament involving entire battalions in Nakfa, just in order to present the image of 'nothing special going on'. Nevertheless, and for unknown reasons, parts of the EPLA's build-up were detected by the Ethiopian military intelligence just a day before the offensive was launched. Correspondingly, the HQ of the II Revolutionary Army warned the Nadew and Manter Commands about an impending enemy assault intended to penetrate deep through Ethiopian lines, and cut off the road between Afabet and Keren. Issued several hours before the start of the Eritrean offensive, this warning still came much too late.[175]

Starting its assault at 0500hrs on 17 March 1988, the 61st Division, EPLA used classic infiltration tactics to isolate Ethiopian positions that offered strong resistance, and progressed rapidly around such points. Nearby, the 70th Division also easily penetrated the Ethiopian forward line and advanced along the Hedai Valley. Before the end of the day, it reached its main objective – the Meshalit Pass – and then forced an isolated Ethiopian Commando battalion to withdraw from this dominating position. This was a tremendous achievement, now the EPLA had cut off the road connection between Afabet and Keren and thus isolated the entire Nadew Command. Finally, the 85th Division, reinforced by mechanized elements of the 74th Heavy-Weapons Division, was the least successful of Eritrean units: it was blocked by fierce resistance from the 29th Mechanized Brigade at Kemchewa until the end of the day.[176]

However, a single brigade of the Ethiopian army was not enough to stop the onslaught of three Eritrean divisions. Under tremendous pressure, and facing the risk of annihilation, the 29th Mechanised Brigade was ordered to withdraw towards Afabet by retreating along the road from Nakfa. The unit formed a convoy of 70 vehicles, mixing trucks, tanks and APCS and set out – with the 85th Division, EPLA, reinforced by a number of captured tanks, in hot pursuit. Disaster struck in the Ad Sharum Pass, the last obstacle before the plains surrounding Afabet, where the 29th Mechanised Brigade would have been far less vulnerable than along the narrow Nakfa-Afabet road. The lead Eritrean T-55 that was following the column managed to destroy the second Ethiopian truck in the front of the column as this reached the top of the pass: the vehicle exploded and blocked the whole convoy, instantly dooming it. Realising their situation, Ethiopian soldiers began to disable their own vehicles with hand grenades, before retreating on foot. After receiving reports about this catastrophe, the MONPC ordered the EtAF to bomb the convoy in order to prevent the insurgents from capturing such a wealth of precious heavy weapons. Overall result of this catastrophe was the demise of one of the most prestigious units of the Ethiopian Army.

This defeat had negative consequences for the victorious Eritreans too: with the Ad Sharum Pass completely jammed with burning hulks, the insurgents were denied the use of the most direct road to Afabet. Correspondingly, the 85th Division was forced to withdraw towards Kemchewa before resuming its advance along the plains separating the Red Sea from the Sahel mountains before turning west again. This delay slowed down the EPLA's advance in other sectors too, because the Eritrean light infantry lacked the firepower to overpower well-defended Ethiopian positions.[177]

Fall of Afabet

Meanwhile, realising the danger for the entire Nadew Command, the MONPC dispatched all available units to dislodge the EPLA's 70th Division from the Mashalit Pass and re-open the Keren-Afabet road. Supported by dozens of EtAF air strikes, the 16th Mechanized Infantry and the 38th Mountain Infantry Brigades attacked this area from the direction of Keren, while the 39th Mountain Infantry Brigade attacked from the direction of Afabet. However, all their assaults failed in the face of fierce insurgent resistance. The 15th Infantry Division was then ordered to dispatch its 78th and 82nd Brigades from Asmara: troops drawn from these two units were transported to Afabet by EtAF helicopters. However, Brigadier-General Wubetu Tsegaye could not move his 102nd Airborne Division because this required permission from the MONPC. Correspondingly, only 650 troops from two brigades of the 15th Infantry Division attacked unsupported, and were quickly thrown back towards Afabet.[178]

Amid complete chaos and disorganisation, the EPLA found it easy to quickly set up the next phase of its offensive. On 19 March 1988 it assaulted Afabet, and by the evening had not only killed the commanders of the 14th and 19th Divisions, but had overcome the last remaining pockets of resistance too. The Ethiopian garrison successfully avoided an encirclement and managed to blow up the HQ of the Nadew Command before withdrawing, but failed to do so in the case of large ammunition depots located in the town. The

Map depicting manoeuvring by major Ethiopian and Eritrean units during the Battle that led to the fall of Afabet in March 1988. (Map by Tom Cooper)

A still from a video showing EPLA troops passing Ethiopian Army tanks and vehicles abandoned or knocked out during the catastrophic defeat of the 29th Mechanized Brigade at the Meshalit Pass. (via Adrien Fontanellaz)

survivors returned to Asmara and Keren – only to find themselves detained by the Military Security: all were isolated and extensively interrogated. Overall, the Ethiopians suffered a loss of 12,116 troops in this battle, including 2,995 killed, 6,038 wounded, and 3,083 missing in action.[179]

Losses were significant on the Eritrean side too, but the EPLA was strongly reinforced by the immense booty of heavy weapons and ammunition. In addition to capturing more than 50 intact armoured vehicles, it also collected several BM-21 MRLs and, for the first time, an unknown number of 130mm M-46 field guns. The latter were to prove a significant addition to the insurgent arsenal because of their long range.

Highly motivated, well trained, ever better equipped, by 1988 Eritrean insurgents were regularly defeating increasingly disorganized and demoralized Ethiopian army units. (Albert Grandolini Collection)

The destruction of the 29th Mechanized Brigade, and the capture of Afabet also proved a major propaganda coup: the EPLF made best use of escorting foreign reporters along the battlefield, and endless photographs of remnants of the 29th Mechanized Brigade's column became symbolic of this war. The insurgents captured three Soviet advisors alive: the appearance of Colonel Evgeny Nikolaevich Cheraev, Colonel Yuri Petrovich Kalistranov, and Lieutenant Aleksander Viktorovich Kuwaldine guaranteed wide media exposure and a major embarrassment for the Soviet Union.[180]

Final Ethiopian Offensive

The victory at Afabet and destruction of the Nadew Command provided the EPLF with other handsome dividends. Instead of following the original plan to adopt a defensive stance after destroying the main Ethiopian military concentration, the insurgents were free to advance on Keren instead, and put the town within range of their reinforced artillery. The II Revolutionary Army reacted by ordering a withdrawal of garrisons of Tesseney, Barentu and Agordat in order to close a giant gap in its frontlines. While in this fashion it managed to concentrate the 2nd Mechanized Division, the 23rd Infantry Division, and the 16th Mechanized Brigade in the Keren area by 2 April 1988, this retreat left the EPLF in control of all of north-western Eritrea and re-establish a land connection to Tigray without a fight.

Over the following weeks, the MONPC continued re-deploying units from all parts of Ethiopia to Eritrea. The 3rd Infantry Division, which was fighting the TPLF in Tigray, was re-deployed to Eritrea, while the 9th Infantry Division moved from Ogaden, by sea, to the Massawa area. None of this was enough to stop the insurgents who were now in high spirits: the EPLA continued pushing towards Keren, and on 8 April 1988 caused heavy losses to the 2nd Mechanized Division. Further exploiting the confusion on the Ethiopian side, the insurgents then rushed two battalions to capture several hills dominating Asmara airport. This prompted a vicious and massive counterattack of the recently arrived 9th Infantry Division and whatever other units the MONPC could collect in this part

of Eritrea – these meanwhile included a total of nine infantry, two mechanized and one airborne division, for a total of 104,791 troops – because an uninterrupted operation of this vital installation was a matter of life and death for Ethiopian military. Realising it was overstretched, the EPLA then resorted to hit-and-run attacks in the Ethiopian rear areas, and deployed the commandos of its small naval arm to raid the port of Assab, on 23 April 1988.[181]

Encouraged by defence successes – no matter how limited these actually were – Mengistu confidently ordered his forces into a large-scale, two-pronged offensive on Afabet. Launched on 17 May 1988, part of the Ethiopian force moved from Keren, and managed to dislodge the insurgents from the Mashalit Pass, but was then stopped by fierce resistance. However, the main effort of this operation came from an entirely unexpected direction. A task force centred around the 102nd Airborne Division, and including up to 90 armoured vehicles, advanced from Massawa along the coastal plain, with the intention of outflanking the Eritreans in the east, before reaching Afabet. The EPLA found itself forced to re-deploy no less than four divisions to counter this threat – which eventually dissipated on its own. Already weakened by weeks of heavy fighting, and extensive marching, the Ethiopians found themselves overcome by the heat while lacking water. Then they began suffering losses: even Brigadier General Temesgen Gemechu, commander of the 102nd Airborne, was killed in an ambush. Eventually, the entire offensive – the last major operation of this kind by Ethiopians in this war – was called off, on 26 May 1988.[182]

With this, the curtain fell over the second phase of the Eritrean Liberation War. Fought since 1961 this conflict lingered for most of its first two decades, but then turned into the biggest conventional war ever fought on the African continent. It did not end with the Eritrean victory at Afabet, in March 1988, but this success of the EPLA marked the beginning of the end – of the Ethiopian hold of Eritrea, and of the Derg government in Addis Ababa. That phase of the war, and subsequent conflicts between Ethiopia and Eritrea are to be covered in the Volume 2 of this mini-series.

BIBLIOGRAPHY

Africa Watch Report, 'Evil Days, 30 years of War and Famine in Ethiopia', September 1991, via www.hrw.org

Amdemichael, Haile Araya, 'East African Crisis Response: Shaping Ethiopian peace force for better participation in future peace operations' (Monterey CA: Naval Postgraduate School thesis, 2006)

Ayele, Fantahun, *The Ethiopian Army: From Victory to Collapse, 1977-1991* (Evanston IL: Northwestern University Press, 2014)

Ayele, Fantahun, 'Operation Flame and the Destruction of the 3rd Division', in *The Ethiopian Journal of Social Sciences* Vol. 1, No. 1, May 2015

Ayele, Fantahun, 'Revisiting history of Gafat : Was emperor Tewodros's military reform an attempt at "translative adaptation" of western technology?' in *African Jounal of History and Culture*, Vol. 8, No. 4, October 2016

Babich, Col Viktor K., 'With Foreigners against Our Own' [in Russian], *Istoriya Aviyatsy* magazine, Volume 25 and 29 [German translation kindly provided by Detlef Billig]

Berhe, Aregawi, 'A Political History of the Tigray People's Liberation Front (1975-1991): Revolt, Ideology and Mobilisation in Ethiopia' (Vrije Universiteit thesis, 2008)

Berri, Capt M., *Aviation in Ethiopia* [*Aviation Be Ethiopia*, in Amharic] (Addis Ababa: Nigd Printing Press, 2002)

Brent, Winston, *African Air Forces* (Nelspruit: Freeworld Publications, 1999)

Clapham, Christopher, *African Guerrillas: Eritrea/Tigray/Sudan/Somalia/Uganda/Rwanda/Congo-Zaire/Liberia/Sierra Leone* (Oxford: James Currey, 1998)

Clapham, Christopher, 'The Ethiopian Coup d'État of December 1960', in *The Journal of Modern African Studies* Vol. 6, No. 4 (December 1968), pp. 495-507.

Connell, Dan, *Against all odds: A Chronicle of the Eritrean Revolution* (Asmara: The Red Sea Press Inc., 1997)

Connell, Dan, *Taking on the Superpowers: Collected Articles on the Eritrean Revolution (1976-1982), Vol.*[1] (Trenton NJ: The Red Sea Press Inc., 2003)

Connell, Dan, *Building a new nation; Collected articles on the Eritrean Revolution (1983-2002) Vol.*[2] (Trenton NJ: The Red Sea Press Inc., 2004)

Cooper, T., Weinert, P., with Hinz, F., and Lepko, M., *African MiGs: MiGs and Sukhois in Service in Sub-Saharan Africa, Volume 1, Angola to Ivory Coast* (Houston TX: Harpia Publishing, 2010)

Cooper, T., Weinert, P., with Hinz, F., and Lepko, M., *African MiGs: MiGs and Sukhois in Service in Sub-Saharan Africa, Volume 2, Madagascar to Zimbabwe* (Houston TX: Harpia Publishing, 2011)

Cooper, T., *Wings over Ogaden: The Ethiopian-Somali War, 1978-79 (Africa@War 18)* (Sollhull, Helion & Company Ltd and Pinetown, 30° South Publishers (Pty) Ltd., 2015)

Director of Central Intelligence Agency, 'The Status of Cuban Military Forces in Ethiopia', Interagency Intelligence Memorandum, 2 September 1981

Eritrea Profile, 'North eastern Sahel Front: From birth to demise Part I' in *Eritrea Profile*, Vol. 21 No. 5, 19 March 2014

Fontrier, Marc, *La chute de la junte militaire éthiopienne, 1987-1991* (Paris : L'Harmattan, 1999, 2007)

Feleke, Zenebe, *It Happened Like That* [*Naber*, in Amharic] (N.p.: printed privately, 2004). The author was imprisoned from 1991 until 1998 and dedicated his publication to a person that helped him smuggle the original of this manuscript out of Ethiopia for publishing.

Flintham, V., *Air Wars and Aircraft: a Detailed Record of Air Combat, 1945 to the Present* (London: Arms and Armour Press, 1989)

Hans, Albert, 'L'armée de Ménélik', in *Revue des Deux Mondes*, Tome 135, 1896

Hilton, Andrew, *The Ethiopian Patriots* (Stroud: Spellmount, 2007)

Hughes, Howard, 'Eine Volksarmee besonderer Art – der Militärkomplex in Eritrea', December 2004

Gorgu, Col Girma, *Let History Speak for Itself* [*Yinager Tariku*, in Amharic] (Miazia: Birhan and Selam Printing Press, 2003)

Jackson, P., 'Death of an Air Force' in *AirForces Monthly* magazine, June 1993

Kotlobovskiy, A. B., *MiG-21 in Local Conflicts* [*MiG-21 v Lokalnih Konfliktah*, in Russian] (Kiev: ArchivPress, 1997)

Lefebvre, Jeffrey A., *Arms for the Horn: U.S. Security Policy in Ethiopia and Somalia, 1953-1991* (University of Pittsburgh Press, 1992)

'Eritreans attack Polish Ship', *Los Angeles Times*, 8 January, 1990,

Marcus, Harold G., *A History of Ethiopia (Updated Edition)* (Berkeley CA: University of California Press, 1994)

Markakis, John, *Ethiopia: The Last Two Frontiers* (Oxford: James Currey, 2011)

May, Clifford D., 'Ethiopian Train Falls off Bridge; 392 are killed', *New York Times*, 15 July 1985

Million Eyob, 'The Anti-colonial Political and Military Struggle Part VII and VIII', 22 March 2013 via www.shabait.com

Möller, Harald, DDR *Äthiopien, Unterstützung für ein Militärregime (1977-1989)* (Berlin: Verlag Dr. Hans-Joachim Köster, 2003)

Mockler, Anthony, *Haile Selassie's War* (Oxford: Signal Books, 2003)

National Photographic interpretation Center, Imagery analysis report, 'Cuban Combat Forces in Ethiopia(S)', January 1981)

Nicolle, David and Ruggieri, Raffaele, *The Italian Invasion of Abyssinia 1935-1936* (Oxford: Osprey Publishing, 2008)

Nkaisserry, Brig Joseph K., *The Ogaden War: An Analysis of its Causes and its Impact on Regional Peace on the Horn of Africa* (Carlisle Barracks PA: Strategic Research Project, US Army War College, 1997)

Pateman, Roy, *Eritrea: Even the stones are burning* (Asmara: The Red Sea Press Inc., 1998)

Pedriali, Ferdinando, *L'Aeronautica Italiana nelle guerre coloniali - Guerra Etiopica 1935-36* (Roma: Ufficio Storico dello Stato Maggiore dell'Aeronautica, 1997), abstracts retrieved via Axis History Forum, 10 February 2017

Pool, David, *From Guerrillas to Government: The Eritrean People's Liberation Front* (Oxford: James Currey, 2001)

Prunier, Gérard, *L'Éthiopie contemporaine* (Paris: Karthala, 2007)

Republic of Korea, Ministry of Patriot and Veterans Affairs, *The Eternal Partnership: Ethiopia and Korea* (n.d.)

Rouquerol, J., 'Premiers enseignements de la guerre d'Abyssinie' in *Revue Militaire Suisse* 81, 1936.

Sarin., Gen O., Dvoretsky, Col L., *Allien Wars: The Soviet Union's Aggressions Against the World, 1919 to 1989* (Novato CA: Presidio Press, 1996)

Schiavon, Max, *Mussolini : un dictateur en guerre* (Paris: Perrin, Paris, 2016)

Scuttts, J., *Northrop F-5/F-20* (Osceola WI: Motorbooks International, 1986)

Shank Ian, 'The Crucible of Combat: Italian Soldier's Perspectives on the Second Italo-Ethiopian War' in *Vanderbilt Historical Review*, Fall 2016

Shifaw, Dawit, *The Diary of Terror: Ethiopia 1974 to 1991* (Victoria B.C.: Trafford Publishing, 2012)

Shinn David H, et al, *Historical Dictionary of Ethiopia* (Lanham MD: Scarecrow Press, 2013)

Tareke, Gebru, *Ethiopia, power & protest, Peasants Revolts in the Twentieth Century* (Asmara: The Red Sea Press Inc., 1996)

Tareke, Gebru, *The Ethiopian Revolution: War in the Horn of Africa* (New Haven CT: Yale University Press, 2009)

Tesfai, Alemseged, *Two Weeks in the Trenches: Reminiscences of Childhood and War in Eritrea* (Asmara: Red Sea Press, 2003)

Uffmann, Milton F., 'Senior Debriefing report: Col Milton F. Uffmann', 4 December 1972

Weldemichael, Awet T., 'The Eritrean Long March: The Strategic Withdrawal of the Eritrean People's Liberation Front (EPLF), 1978-1979', in *The Journal of Military History* Volume 73 (October 2009)

Young, John, 'The Tigray and Eritrean People's Liberation Fronts: A History of Tensions and Pragmatism', in *The Journal of Modern African Studies*, Volume 34, Number 1, 1996

Zambon, David, 'Duce contre Negus', in *Ligne de Front* No. 65, January-February 2017

Interviews with various participants (see acknowledgements and endnotes); various articles in publications as mentioned in endnotes.

NOTES

Chapter 1

1. Addis Ababa was established as Ethiopian capital in 1886, in Intoto Valley, in course of Menelik IV's attempts to re-unite the country, see Marcus, *A History of Ethiopia*, pp. 104-116.
2. Ibid, pp. 104-116. The concession for railways was issued to a French company in 1894; construction of the stretch from Djibouti to Dire Dawa – a town some 45km from Harar – was completed on 31 December 1902.
3. Ayelle, 2016, pp. 5-11&Albert Hans (see Bibliography for details).
4. Ayelle, 2016, pp. 5-11; John Markakis, p. 123; Historical Dictionary, p. 227.
5. For a detailed history of the Ethiopian Air Force, see Volume 18 of the Africa@War Series, *Wings over Ogaden*.
6. Nicolle, pp. 13-14 & Albert Hans.
7. Nicolle, pp. 13-14.
8. Albert Hans.
9. Hilton, p. 81.
10. Ibid, p. 14 &Albert Hans.
11. Mockler, p. 85.
12. Zambon & Nicolle, pp. 22-24.
13. Schiavon, pp. 71-72.
14. Ibid, p. 73 & Rouquerol RMS.
15. Based on Nicolle, pp. 41-42 & Zambon et al. Notable is that the two 13,200-strong Eritrean units had less firepower than their continental counterparts, but proved highly effective because of their fighting spirit and mobility in mountainous terrain. Furthermore, Italian officers found it opportune to limit casualties among their own troops, and thus tended to deploy the Eritreans as shock troops.
16. Mockler, p. 56; Zambon & Ferdinando Pedriali via Axis History Forum (extracted 10 February 2017).
17. Zambon; Nicolle, p. 8; Mockler, pp. 61-63 & Schiavon, pp. 74-75.
18. Cooper, pp. 7-10.
19. Shank, p. 21.
20. Hilton, p. 62.
21. Mockler, pp. 81-84 & Shanks, p. 20.
22. Zambon & Mockler, pp. 96-103.
23. Ibid, pp. 104-106.
24. Mockler, pp. 108-110.
25. Ibid, pp. 113-116 & 410.
26. Zambon; Mockler, pp. 116-119 & 121.
27. Zambon.
28. Ibid & Mockler, pp. 68-69 & 89.
29. Zambon; Mockler, pp. 89-93; Nicolle, p. 10.
30. Zambon; Mockler, pp. 128-129; Nicolle, p. 10.
31. Mockler, pp. 109, 120, 127 & 129.
32. Ibid, pp. 127 & 136; Nicolle, p. 10.
33. Mockler, pp. 152-173.
34. Ibid, pp. 174-177; Hilton, pp. 43-44 & 63.
35. Hilton, pp. 37 & 45.

Chapter 2

36. Ayele, 2014, pp. 5-11.
37. Tareke, 1996, pp. 92-100.
38. Ibid, pp. 100, 106-108.
39. Ibid, pp. 109-120.
40. Markakis, p. 123 & Ayele, pp. 5-11.
41. Ayele, 2014, pp. 10, 18, 60, 85.
42. According to contemporary US reports, average Ethiopian Army units of this period were usually slightly smaller than units of comparable size in Western armies. For example: a company had on average between 90 and 120 officers and other ranks; a battalion between 300 and 400, and a brigade between 2,000 and 3,000. See, 'Senior Debriefing Report: Col Milton F. Uffamann', 4 December 1972. According to Ayele (p. 60), this practice remained in force during the Derg-regime of the 1980s.
43. Ayele, pp. 10-11.
44. Cooper, p. 12 & Techane Zewdie interview, 2006. Notably, the Ethiopian military build-up of the 1950s, 1960s, and early 1970s was described in much more detail in Volume 18 of the Africa@War Series, *Wings over Ogaden*. For example, the fleet of F-86Fs was further increased through donation of six ex-US Air National Guard examples, and 10 ex-Imperial Iranian Air Force Sabres to the IEAF in 1970, enabling the air force to establish its fourth fighter-interceptor squadron. Techane was one of IEAF pilots to test-fly F-86Fs transferred from Iran, and he recalled that these were flown to Ethiopia from Dezful via Riyadh to Debre Zeit. Later on, Techane was re-assigned to 5th Squadron, where he flew former Iranian Northrop F-5As.
45. Lefebvre, p. 90.
46. Ibid, p. 95. For details of the coup attempt, see Cooper, pp. 12-13. Notable is that not only were numerous of involved officers

and other ranks subsequently jailed (and its commander, Brigadier General Mangestu Neway executed), but the Imperial Body Guard was decreased in size to a brigade-sized unit, while surplus personnel was re-distributed to various other units of the IEA.

47. Lefebvre, p. 95; Fontrier, pp. 506-512; Ayele 2014, pp. 9-11 & 33; Tareke, p. 114 & Cooper, pp. 11-13 & 15-20
48. Ayele 2014, pp. 13 & 33; Cooper, pp. 15-20; SIPRI (extracted 14 August 2005).
49. Prunier, p. 138.
50. Ibid, p. 137.
51. Ibid, p. 139; Fontrier, p. 507 & Tareke, p. 38.
52. Prunier, p. 139.
53. Cooper, pp. 25-28; Fontrier, pp. 507-509; Prunier, p. 141 & Tareke, pp. 38-42 & 117.
54. Prunier, pp. 142-143.
55. Ayele 2014, p. 11 & Cooper, p. 15.
56. Tareke, pp. 125-150.
57. Ayele, pp. 27 & 102-103; Cooper, pp. 27-31 & Tareke, p. 188.
58. Pool, pp. 26-36 & Connell, p. 76.
59. Donnell, p. 76; Pateman, pp. 98 & 118; Pool, pp. 50-73; 'Senior Debriefing Report: Col Milton F Uffmann', 4 December 1972.
60. Pool, p. 51 & Pateman, p. 118.
61. Tareke, p. 113.
62. Ayele 2014, pp. 23-24 & Pateman, p. 97.
63. 'Senior Debriefing Report: Col Milton F Uffmann', 4 December 1972.
64. Pool, pp. 53-64.
65. Cooper, p. 19.
66. Connell, pp. 82-83 & Pool, pp. 70 & 74-78.
67. Ibid & Flintham, pp. 146-147.

Chapter 3

68. Pateman, pp. 79-81 & 134.
69. Ibid, pp. 80 & 134 & Pool, p. 137.
70. Ayele 2014, pp. 29, 104, 127 & Tareke, pp. 178-179.
71. Connell, p. 165.
72. Ayele 2014, pp. 127-133 & Connell, p. 94.
73. Pool, p. 140.
74. Connell, p. 96 & Pateman, p. 134.
75. Connell, pp. 95-97 & Pool, p. 139.
76. Pool, pp. 84-85 & Tareke, p. 66.
77. Pool, pp. 119 & 130 & Tareke, pp. 68-69.
78. Hughes, p. 11 & Tareke, p. 67.
79. Hughes, p. 4; Pool pp. 95-98 & Tareke, p. 70.
80. Hughes, p. 7.
81. Ibid, p. 10; Pool, p. 152, Tareke, p. 73.
82. Pateman, p. 124; Pool, p. 150 & Young, pp. 109-110.
83. 'North-Eastern Sahel Front: From Birth to Demise, Part 1', *Eritrea Profile*, Volume 21, No. 5 (19 March 2014).
84. Hughes, pp. 70-71.
85. Ibid, pp. 8-14.
86. Pool, pp. 98 & 102 & Tareke, pp. 71-74.
87. Clapham, 1998, p. 38; Berhe, pp. 81-82 & Tareke, p. 84.
88. Berhe, pp. 93-94, 105-107 & 170 & Tareke, p. 96.
89. Berhe, p. 100 & Tareke, p. 86.
90. Berhe, pp. 125-130 & Tareke, pp. 86-87.
91. Berhe, pp. 132-135 & Tareke, p. 87.
92. Berhe, pp. 147-150 & Tareke, p. 88. History can often be as ironic as almost sarcastic. This is most obvious from the fact that the rivalries between Eritrean insurgents had consequences on the Ethiopian insurgent scene – and then in most unexpected fashion.

Not only that the EPLF's support for the TPLF prompted the ELF to support the TLA, but the leftist EPRP supported even the monarchist Ethiopian Democratic Union. Furthermore, the TPLF's build-up and elimination of its rivals were immensely helped by the Derg, which spent much of the 1970s destroying various other movements while failing to react against the nascent, yet far more dangerous movement. Indeed, for most of the 1980s, Addis Ababa concentrated most of its attention at the EPLF, while considering Tigray a 'side show'.

93. Berhe, p. 120 & Clapham 1998, pp. 42-43.
94. Ayele, p. 166; Berhe, pp. 105-106 & 120; Fontrier, p. 77 & Tareke, p. 98. Sources differ widely over the TPLF's manpower and order of battle, and in regards of distinguishing between its regular units and local militias. Certain is only that during the last years of the war this movement could mobilize large number of combatants and run conventional operations.
95. Berhe, p. 234.
96. Fontrier, p. 79 & Tareke, p. 93.
97. Young, p. 111.

Chapter 4

98. Ayele 2014, pp. 37 & 76; Tareke, p. 119.
99. Ayele 2014, pp. 29-30, 56-60 & 117; Tareke, p. 120.
100. Ayele 2014, pp. 57 & 61, 145-146 & 188; Tareke, p. 120. Notable is that some of newly-established brigades had honorary designations like the 16th 'Santeq', and the 29th 'Zara'y Daras'.
101. Ayele 2014, pp. 30, 34, 38 & 56.
102. Tareke, pp. 137 & 157.
103. Ibid, pp. 149-153.
104. Subsequent statistics collected by the Ethiopian Ministry of National Defence estimated that the nation lost more than 400,000 soldiers killed or missing in action between 1974 and 1990, see Tareke, pp. 126 & 132.
105. Ayele 2014, p. 35 & Tareke, pp. 130-131.
106. Ayele 2014, pp. 35-36 & Tareke, pp. 128-129.
107. Tareke, pp. 123-126; Fontrier, p. 58 & Ayele 2014, p. 59.
108. Tareke, p. 168.
109. Ayele 2014, p. 62.
110. Ayele 2014, pp. 77-80 & Tareke, pp. 144-146.
111. Ayele 2014, p. 75.
112. Tareke, p. 121 & Ayele 2014, p. 210.
113. Tareke, p. 121 & Fontrier, pp. 513-514.
114. Fontrier, pp. 62-63.
115. National Photographic Interpretation Center, 'Cuban Combat Forces in Ethiopia (S)', *CIA Eletronic Reading Room* (January 1981).
116. Ibid & Fontrier, pp. 63-64.
117. Tareke, pp. 134-137 & 375; Ayele 2014, pp. 70 & 211.
118. Ayele 2014, p. 50 & Fontrier, p. 61.
119. Berhanu Wubneh interview, 2008. This and all subsequent quotations from Berhanu are based on transcriptions of the same interview.
120. Except for Lieutenant Colonel Hailemikael Birru, the first group of Ethiopian pilots to convert to MiG-21s included Major Teshale Zewdie (ex-F-5A-pilot), Major Tesfu Desta (F-5A), Captain Ambachew Wube (F-5A), Captain Ashenafi Gebre Tsadik (F-5E), Captrain Wagari Gemechu (F-86), Lietenants Tilahun Bogale and Mengesha Hunde (F-86 and Safir pilots, respectivelly), and 2nd Lieutenants Alemayehu Haile and Berhanu Demissie. The second group included Lieutenant Colonel Gizaw Diriba (F-86), Major Berhanu Wubneh (F-5E), Major Neguissie Zergaw (F-5A), Captain Tilahun Woldemariam (F-5A), Captain Alemayehu Kebede (F-

86), Captain Getachew Tekle-Giorgis (F-86), Lieutenant Nebiyu Abraha (F-5A), and 2nd Lieutenants Kinfu Habtewolde (F-86), Getachew Mengesha and Hilina Mammo.

121. Cooper, pp. 47-49. At the time of the Somali invasion, a group of eleven Ethiopian F-5 and F-86 pilots – including Ashenafi Gebre Tsadik, Berhanu Wubneh and Teshale Zewdie – led by Lieutenant Colonel Haile Michael Birru (who previously served as the commander of Dire Dawa AB), were undergoing a four-months conversion training on MiG-21s in the USSR. When the Somalis invaded, they had finished ground training and were ready to take their exams: completing these without any problems, they returned to Ethiopia only in late August 1977. The second group of Ethiopian pilots – all of them former F-86 fliers – was also in the USSR by the time of the Somali invasion.

122. Ibid, p. 49.

123. Ashenafi interview, 2001.

124. Tareke, pp. 121 & 374; SIPRI Trade Register (extracted 9 September 2015).

125. Shifaw, pp. 129-134.

Chapter 5

126. Connell, pp. 113-115.

127. Ibid, pp. 116, 127, 147 & 155.

128. Ibid, pp. 141-144.

129. Ibid, pp. 150-154.

130. Ayele 2014, pp. 56 & 75; Tareke, p. 179 & Berghe, p. 177.

131. Ayele 2014, p. 134 & Awet T. Wekdenichael.

132. Berghe, pp. 177-178; Connell, pp. 159 & Awet T. Wekdenichael.

133. Connell, pp. 244-254 & 273-275.

134. Flintham, p. 147; Connell, p. 297; Ayele, p. 134 & *North Eastern Sahel Front: From Birth to Demise, Part I.*

135. Ayele 2014, p. 134, Connell, p. 303.

136. Ayele 2014, p. 134; Connell, p. 299.

137. Connell, pp. 303, 359 & 364.

138. Connell, p. 174, Ayele, p. 135 & *North Eastern Sahel Front: From Birth to Demise, Part I.*

139. Awet T. Wekdenichael.

140. Ibid.

141. Connell, pp. 202-208 & Pool, pp. 146-147.

142. Ayele 2014, pp. 32 & 66; Tareke, pp. 220-225 & 240; Cooper, pp. 56-57.

143. Ayele 2014, pp. 32 & 66-67; Berhe, pp. 181-182.

Chapter 6

144. Ayele 2014, pp. 56-57 & pp. 138-139; Tareke, pp. 231-232 & Connel, p. 217.

145. Ayele 2014, pp. 138-139; Tareke, pp. 228-229; Pateman, p. 127.

146. Connell, pp. 532-533; *North Eastern Sahel Front: From Birth to Demise, Part I.*

147. Young, p. 107. In comparison, Berhe (p. 257) explicitly states that the TPLF deployed three of its brigades to Eritrea – *after* the start of the Ethiopian offensive, and then with explicit intention of helping the Eritreans during the Operation Red Star.

148. Ayele 2014, pp. 138-139 & Connel, pp. 532-533.

149. Alternative reports cite this aircraft as crashing near Addis Ababa in what was the worst aircraft disaster in Ethiopia of all times.

150. Ayele 2014, pp. 138-139; Connell, pp. 535-542; Pateman, pp. 138-139 & Flintham, p. 147. Figures cited here are those based on Ethiopian sources. The EPLF originally claimed the destruction of 32 aircraft, including 16 MiG-23s, 2 An-26s, two 'bombers', four 'other aircraft', and 6 Mi-8 and Mi-24 helicopters. However, there

is no evidence for such a massive loss of EtAF aircraft – regardless if at this, or any other, date during this war.

151. Ayele 2014, p. 139; Tareke, p. 232; Flintham, p. 147.

152. Ayele 2014, pp. 57, 67, 139-141 & 145; Tareke, pp. 232-233.

153. Ayele 2014, pp. 139-140; Tareke, pp. 232-234, 237-238.

154. Ayele 2014, pp. 139-140, Tareke, pp. 232-238.

155. Ayele 2014, p. 141; Tareke, pp. 234-235.

156. Ayele 2014, p. 141. This measure was actually less desperate than it might appear, then the EPLF's standard practice was to provide basic military training to all of its members, including those who never enrolled in the EPLA.

157. Ayele 2014, p. 141; Tareke, pp. 234-235.

158. Ayele 2014, pp. 141-144; Tareke, pp. 238-241.

159. Ayele 2014, p. 145; Tareke, p. 245.

Chapter 7

160. Berhe, pp. 183, 267-270; Tareke, p. 95.

161. Berhe, pp. 267-270; Tareke, p. 96; Young, pp. 112-116.

162. Ayele 2014, p. 145; Pateman, p. 141. EtAF suffered a heavy loss during the same month too. On 16 February 1984, a disgruntled soldier hijacked an An-12B transport (serial 1509) during a flight to Asmara. Using a hand-grenade, the hijacker demanded to be flown to Sudan. The crew turned back to Debre Zeit AB instead, but the hijacker then detonated the hand grenade, causing the aircraft to crash, killing all 26 on board.

163. Ashenafi Gebre Tsadik, interview, 2001. This and all subsequent quotations from Ashenafi are based on transcriptions of the same interview.

164. All five F-5Es were overhauled, completely restored and returned to service with the IRIAF, where they received serials from 3-7182 to 3-7186. Eight F-5As were restored too, and they originally served as advanced, single-seat trainers, with serials from 2-7250 to 2-7257. Since mid-1990s, most of F-5As in question were re-worked to the indigenous Iranian variant named Saeqeh: i.e. converted into two-seat conversion trainers.

165. Ayele 2014, pp. 93-94; 145-146 & 150-151; Pateman, p. 144. As so often, the EPLF subsequently published wildly exaggerated claims for number of aircraft destroyed in these two raids. For example, after the attack of 14 January 1986, it reported no less than 40 blown up.

166. Ayele 2014, p. 146. Notable is that according to Ethiopian documentation, the army suffered no less than 5,617 casualties on 5 and 6 July 1985 alone. Of these, 1,389 troops were killed, 2,476 wounded, and 1,752 went missing in action.

167. Patman (p. 143) cites the re-deployment of the 5th Mechanized Division from Ogaden. However, it is more likely that the Derg sent the recently established 2nd Mechanized Division instead.

168. Reports by New York Times, 15 July 1985; Ayele, pp. 71 & 146; Pateman, pp. 142-143; Tareke, pp. 180 & 248-249; Milion Eyob, The Anti-colonial Political and Military Struggle, Part VII (22 March 2013) <http://www.shabait.com>

169. According to Ayele (p. 148) most of these were caused by deliberate sabotage.

170. Ayele, pp. 57-58 & 146-152; Pateman, p. 144 & Milion Eyob, The Anti-colonial Political and Military Struggle, Part VII (22 March 2013) <http://www.shabait.com>

171. Ayele 2014, p. 152; Tareke, pp. 248-249; Dawit, p. 151.

172. Tareke, pp. 250-251; Ayele, p. 153.

173. Ayele 2014, pp. 153-154; Tareke, pp. 251-252.

174. Ayele 2014, pp. 59 & 154; Tareke, p. 253.

175. Ayele 2014, pp.154-155; Tareke, p. 253; Tesfai, pp. 99-101.

176. Tareke, p. 254; Tesfai, pp. 99-112.
177. Ayele 2014, p. 155; Tareke, pp. 254-255; Tesfai, pp. 120-121.
178. Ayele 2014, pp. 75 & 155-156; Tareke, p. 256.
179. Ayele 2014, p. 156.
180. Ayele 2014, p. 156; Tareke, p. 256; Tesfai, p. 122; Shifaw, pp. 151-152; Fontier, p. 138 & Pateman, p. 146.
181. Ayele 2014, pp. 157-158; Tareke, pp. 258-259; Pateman, p. 146; Shifaw, pp. 152-155.
182. Ayele 2014, pp. 157-158; Tareke, pp. 258-259; Pateman, p. 146; Shifaw, pp. 152-155; Fontier, p. 139.

ABOUT THIS BOOK

Ethiopia, a country of ancient origins in eastern Africa, remains a military powerhouse of that continent until our days. Nowadays involved in the war in neighbouring Somalia, Ethiopia was also involved in half a dozen of other armed conflicts over the last 60 years. Crucial between these was the Eritrean War of Independence. Fought 1961-1991, this was one of biggest armed conflicts on the African continent, especially if measured by numbers of involved combatants. It included a wide spectrum of operations, from 'classic' counter-insurgency (COIN) to conventional warfare in mountains – with the latter being one of the most complex and most demanding undertakings possible to conduct by a military force. Campaigns run during the Eritrean War of Independence often included large formations of relatively well-equipped forces, led by well-trained commanders, along well-thought-out plans, based on home-grown doctrine. The air power played a crucial – although not necessarily decisive – role in many of battles. Nevertheless, most of details about this conflict remain unknown in the wider public. Similarly, relatively few Western observers are aware of relations between the Eritrean liberation movements, and various dissident and insurgent movements inside Ethiopia – although the synergy of these eventually led the downfall of the so-called Derg government, in 1991. Reaching back on extensive studies of Ethiopian and Eritrean military history, this volume is providing a detailed account of the first 25 years of this conflict: from the outbreak of armed insurgency in 1961 until the crucial battle of Afabet, in 1988. It is illustrated by over 100 contemporary photographs, maps and 15 colour profiles.

ABOUT THE AUTHORS

Adrien Fontanellaz

Adrien Fontanellaz, from Switzerland, is a military history researcher and author. He developed a passion for military history at an early age and has progressively narrowed his studies to modern-day conflicts. He is a member of the Scientific Committee of the Pully-based Centre d'histoire et de prospective militaires (Military History and Prospective Centre), and regularly contributes for the Revue Militaire Suisse and various French military history magazines. He is co-founder and a regular contributor to the French military history website *L'autre coté de la colline*, and this is his third title for Helion's '@War' series.

Tom Cooper

Tom Cooper is an Austrian aerial warfare analyst and historian. Following a career in a worldwide transportation business – during which he established a network of contacts in the Middle East and Africa – he moved into narrow-focus analysis and writing on small, little-known air forces and conflicts, about which he has collected extensive archives. This has resulted in specialisation in such Middle Eastern air forces as those of Egypt, Iran, Iraq and Syria, plus various African and Asian air forces. As well as authoring and co-authoring more than 30 books - including an in-depth analysis of major Arab air forces at wars with Israel during the period 1955-1973 - and over 1,000 articles, Cooper is a regular correspondent for multiple specialised defence-related publications.